BE ON GUARD.

A PROVEN Path to Sexual Integrity

Straightforward help with issues of lust,
pornography, masturbation or other forms of
sexual addiction from a Biblical perspective

Joel Hesch

Published and printed in the U.S.A. by Proven Men Ministries, Ltd., Lynchburg, Virginia

First Edition

ISBN: 978-1-940011-01-1

Proven Men, Proven Man, Proven Path, Proven Life, and the PROVEN term and acronym are protected trademarks and service marks of Joel Hesch.

Details in stories or anecdotes have been changed to protect the identities of the persons involved.

Interior Design: 1106 Design

Cover Design: Prototype

Hesch, Joel

PROVEN MEN: A PROVEN Path to Sexual Integrity; Straightforward help with issues of lust, pornography, masturbation or other forms of sexual addiction from a Biblical perspective / Joel Hesch.

1. Sex—Religious aspects—Christianity. 2. Temptation. 3. Christian men—Religious life. 4. Sexual Health Recovery.

Acknowledgments

This book is dedicated to my lovely wife, Theresa, for her faithfulness and support. She never gave up on me even though she had every right to! I am grateful that she believes in and trusts me like never before. She has also been such a great support to so many wives as they faced similar tough times as their husbands were transitioning into Proven Men.

I also dedicate this book to my dad, who became my biggest cheerleader in life. Before he died, I was able to talk to him about my childhood issues and make peace with him. More importantly, through our open and honest discussions, he placed his trust in Jesus as Lord of his life at the age of 72. He is now in heaven waiting for me and my family.

I also acknowledge my two closest Networking Partners, Pastor Steve Pettit and Brian Hall. They are more than brothers in the Lord—they became my dearest allies and partners in ministry. I couldn't have written this book, founded Proven Men Ministries, Ltd., or lived a Proven life without them.

I am also grateful for the two churches that I attended since becoming a Proven Man. They each knew me and still loved me. Both Brentwood Church in Lynchburg, Virginia, and Derwood Bible Church in Rockville, Maryland, saw Christ in me instead of my past and each invited me to get off the bench and get into the game serving in the spiritual role of church elder.

Passionate for God,
Repentant in spirit,
Open and honest,
Victorious in living,
Eternal in perspective, and
Networking with other *Proven Men.*

Table of Contents

PROVENMEN™
BE ON GUARD.

Passionate for God,
Repentant in spirit,
Open and honest,
Victorious in living,
Eternal in perspective, and
Networking with other *Proven Men.*

Preface: Author's Story and Reason for This Book

Our nation, and indeed the entire world, is crying out for Godly men to lead us through the coming century. Sadly, however, most good men are benchwarmers. They're afraid to lead or even dream big dreams, because they fear that they've somehow been disqualified by the secret issues with sexual sin they foster in their hearts. Many of these men are even afraid of leading their own families. The truth is most men are living defeated, ineffective lives.

That used to be me.

My story is like so many other ordinary men. I struggled with the same sexual temptations as every single or married man. Actually I did more than struggle; I gave in. As a single, I engaged in premarital sex, viewed pornography and was addicted to masturbation. To my horror, my lustful thought life and addiction to masturbation did not simply go away when I invited Jesus into my heart at age 25. It did not go away when I got married at 27. In an act of defeat, I resigned myself to the fact that I must live a secret, double agent life. So I sat on the bench, believing I was disqualified to be a leader, at least as to spiritual or other matters that depended on the condition of my heart.

My secret life failed to produce the desired results. Daily I was riddled with guilt and shame. I was fearful that my wife would find me out and leave. I was afraid the church would discover and shun me.

My protective plan was to hide—and hide so deep no one would ever know the real me. I even swore an oath that I would take to the grave my dirty little secret that I masturbated. At any cost, I was willing to lie—to deny that I masturbated. It was that dark of a secret.

On the other hand, on the outside, I had everything. I graduated fifth in my D.C. law school class and soon landed a prestigious job. At church I was asked to lead Bible studies and small groups. I was also the chairman of the Trustees and helped head the building committee. As to my home life, my wife was gorgeous, not just in my mind, but she had titles of cheerleader and prom queen. But there was a scary part about her. She was working as the family and marriage counselor at our church. That meant, gulp, she was very perceptive; so I needed to be even better at hiding.

Seven years into my marriage, however, my two worlds collided. Yes, I was still feeding an active fantasy life and almost daily masturbating, but that was not worst of it. I began crossing lines in the sand—lines that even I knew not to cross. I had justified my thought life by also vowing never to have a physical affair. I would not commit adultery. But I was finding myself flirting with real women. I even began entertaining the thought that I would act out one of my sexual fantasies. I was no longer able to keep the wild animal of lust in the cage of my mind. Then it happened. One day I actually asked a woman to have sex with me! Fortunately, she said no.

In a flash, I came to my senses. I was just an inch away from adultery—the real physical form of adultery when you sleep with another person. Looking back, I couldn't believe how many times I had kept moving the line farther and farther away from purity and integrity. I was scared because an affair would likely end my marriage, and I truly loved my wife.

I was in desperate need of help. I couldn't go on living a lie. But I couldn't win the battle on my own. I didn't want to throw away my marriage. I wanted—no, I needed—to stop living two lives. If I didn't tell someone right away, guilt, shame and fear would grip me again and I would crawl back to my hiding place and forever remain a prisoner. Having nothing to lose and nowhere else to turn, I drove to my pastor's house and told him my entire story.

The moment of reckoning was upon me. I waited anxiously for a response. I was ready for judgment and rejection. As I stared into Pastor Steve's eyes, tears began to flow down his face. He rose. I froze.

It seemed like an eternity before he walked up to me. I heard a soft whisper in my ear as he put his arms around my shoulders. He simply said, "Joel, I love you."

I was stunned. I was unable to think or speak. I couldn't even hug him back. As he sat down again, I just stared at him. He continued, "It sounds like you have an addiction."

As he paused for a second, I chimed in, "I don't care what you call it … I need help!"

With a calm and reassuring voice, he told me he didn't know how to address sexual integrity problems, but that he would find out and he would walk every step with me. All I could say back was, "Please hurry!"

I immediately went home and confessed everything to my wife. I had to watch tears stream from her eyes. It killed me to witness her heart break. Although it was the hardest thing I ever had to do, it was also the most liberating moment of my life. The weight of shame was immediately lifted. I had no more secrets. I felt what it could be like to be free. I felt hope. I didn't know if my wife would stay with me, but I knew that I would never turn back to my secret double life. From that day forward, I was going to live for the Lord, not myself.

The next thing that happened was something I could have only dreamed of. My wife told me that she would not leave me but that we would work on it together. It ended up being a hard and long process, but for the first time we began acting as partners and started having a real marriage.

Both of the lies of Satan that had kept me in bondage were defeated. Neither my church nor my wife disowned me. I was finally free to be the man God created me to be.

Of course, there was much work ahead. I had years of backward thinking to undo. I had many habits to break. I also needed to replace all of these selfish practices for thoughts pure, lovely and admirable. I needed to allow myself to experience feelings and be open in my relationships.

From that day forward, I never looked at pornography and never masturbated. I felt as if I had been tested and stamped PROVEN by the Lord.

Three years later, I was called to reach out to men in my church. If I made a vow of silence and hid, I knew others did too. I shared my story at men's functions and retreats and began meeting with men who faced similar struggles. I began writing a study to guide men to freedom and started leading small support groups.

My journey toward freedom and victory formed the basis for Proven Men Ministries, Ltd. For more than ten years, I've been offering the same comfort that I received to others as they battle and war with sexual sins. This book is my battle cry for all men to join with me and all men in the fight for sexual integrity. It's a culmination of what I have personally learned from the Lord and from connecting with many other Proven Men who are now living victorious lives.

My heart aches for men sitting silently while trapped by the guilt and shame associated with sexual sin. It saddens me to know that millions of men are closing themselves off from others just as I had for fear of being rejected or unable to measure up. So I feel compelled to rise up and speak, to link arms with other Proven Men. Won't you accept the invitation to stand with me—with us—linked together through modern day networking with kindred spirits, united in heart and purpose to live out a Proven life? In your struggle for purity, you're no longer alone.

My Dream

I have a dream. I see a nation—and a world—where every man claims his own sexual integrity and, when he is tested, he stands firm. Imagine the impact of millions of men throwing off the shackles of guilt and shame that are holding them back and rising up to be leaders. That's my dream.

And it begins with you. If every man is to be a bastion of sexual integrity, it begins one man at a time. It begins with small steps. It begins by you—and every one of us—knowing and living out our true purpose in life. It begins by joining our hands and hearts as we together climb God's holy mountain, encouraging each other along the way. No more secret lives. No more double agents.

In my vision the brotherhood of Proven Men arises to follow God's plan. We stop sitting on the sidelines and boldly ask God to put us back in the game. It's time to push aside everything that hinders or holds us back. Only then can we achieve purity and restoration to achieve God's precious promise of enduring contentment and joy.

Allow this book to be your road map, a reliable set of basic principles and a path to follow so you can lead a Proven life. It will show you how to link arms with others who have experienced dashed hopes and real fears, but now experience a better place that's holy and just.

In the first steps of this journey as I ministered to many men, some told me it feels as if the scales have fallen from their eyes—finally allowing them to see and follow God's plan for sexual integrity. Others have torn down huge walls they built during childhood and have come to experience true intimacy with the Lord or their spouses for the first time. I have torn down my last remaining wall and am publicly sharing my story and finally crushing the bondage of secrecy.

As you link with us, please know that the journey is not identical for each man. God meets you where you are. He brings you along at a speed you can handle. Just as the stories in this book of Joel, Tim and Stan are different, so is yours. But we are all part of the same team, striving for the same goal.

It's time to shed your former ways of thinking about sexual integrity and prepare yourself to experience healing and freedom from the Lord. God will impart His wisdom and strength. He will grant you victory. But you must be willing to do it His way this time.

There's so much more I want to share. But for now, allow me to invite you to go on a journey—a Proven Path every man must take as he strives for sexual integrity. Won't you join with me, as I join others in a brotherhood of Proven Men?

Introduction: Understanding the Purpose of This Book

Let me say up front that this book is not a self-help book. It's the opposite. In fact, I can personally guarantee you that your own efforts will ultimately fail, just as I failed over and over again for 20 years of acting alone and in my own strength. Living purely isn't about tugging harder at your bootstraps to pull yourself up out of the miry pit. You can try it, but it won't work. Neither is it about following a catchy set of self-help tips that promise to put a stop to lusting or looking at pornography. Man-made programs are not capable of lasting results, because they don't address the root issue that gives life to impurity.

This book pushes aside the typical misconceptions about sexual integrity. It will be your guide to unlocking the mystery of becoming a Proven Man in the midst of an era with a worldview based on sex. But, make no mistake. There are no shortcuts and no magic formulas. Of course, reading this book may not instantly change you. But it does give you a Proven Path to follow. As you'll soon learn, sexual integrity is actually a *by-product of a right relationship with God.* Victory will be won through living out six fundamentals of our Christian faith, on which the PROVEN acronym is based and more fully explained later. It begins with guarding your heart, so be on guard.

Here's the way this book is organized and how to get the most out of it. Plan to read the first 12 chapters in order because they build upon each other.

Part I contains four chapters explaining the nature of sexual immorality and why it causes us to hide. You need to grasp what you're escaping from in order to make a clean break.

Part II covers the fundamentals and introduces the Proven Path. Because these four chapters are the foundations, avoid the temptation to skim or skip ahead even if some parts seem basic.

Part III tells you how to become a Proven Man in the area of sexual integrity. There's a lot packed in these four chapters, and you may need to read through it a few times.

In addition, there are five appendices addressing special issues. First, Appendix A speaks to whether and why Jesus is the only answer. If you aren't so sure why we consider Jesus an essential part of the equation, feel free to read Appendix A before reading this book.

Second, Appendix B boldly addresses a hot topic of masturbation. It tackles whether it is a sin and how to break its grip.

Third, Appendix C suggests how a husband or fiancé should break the news of lapses in sexual integrity.

Fourth, Appendix D takes it one step further by providing guidance for wives (or fiancées) in reaction to your confession of your sexual sin. The first part contains some practical advice. Since I cannot speak from a woman's perspective, I have asked my wife to explain what this experience is like from her own point of view, since she has gone through this and weathered the storm. Her words are directed to your wives and partners. The last part is a statement by the author of this book, speaking both as a husband who has wounded his wife and as a purity small group leader for other men who are striving to break free from the grip of sexually addictive behaviors. Plan to share Appendix D (and indeed this entire book) with your wife or fiancée. It can help you initiate open and honest conversations about life issues—especially such a sensitive topic as sexual integrity.

Finally, Appendix E consists of the full, reprinted stories of Joel, Tim and Stan that are used throughout this book. They are combined there to allow you to read them from start to finish for each man. They are based upon real stories of real Proven Men. Hopefully they will be a source of encouragement.

Ready to begin? It's time to be on guard and join a brotherhood of Proven Men.

Passionate for God,
Repentant in spirit,
Open and honest,
Victorious in living,
Eternal in perspective, and
Networking with other *Proven Men.*

PART I
THE NATURE OF IMMORALITY

Passionate for God,
Repentant in spirit,
Open and honest,
Victorious in living,
Eternal in perspective, and
Networking with other *Proven Men.*

Chapter 1

Our Sex-Charged Society

In the early fifties, Hollywood portrayed the sex addict as a weak man in a raincoat with shifty eyes. He worked at a job paying minimum wage and spent his time in seedy parts of town, skulking into adult porn shops and XXX-rated films.

Times have changed. Today Hollywood glorifies sex and even what we would consider sexual addiction. Some of the most glamorous male stereotypes, such as James Bond, are known for seducing women. Few, if any, are one-woman men. Today, in fact, it's hard to think of any popular prime-time television shows where premarital and even extramarital affairs are not only common place, but esteemed. Television shows depict sexual adultery scenes twice as often as sex between married couples,[1] and they present "alternative" sexual behaviors, such as voyeurism, incest, prostitution, homosexuality, three times as often as sex in marriage.[2]

The fallout from our sex-charged society is that sex addiction has become commonplace. Ten percent of men in America acknowledge they are flat-out addicted to sex or Internet pornography.[3] More than 25 million spend 1 to 10 hours per week viewing Internet pornography, and 5 million more are spending over 11 hours per week.[4] Sixty-five percent of those addicted to sex are professionals with a college or graduate degree.[5]

What about men in the church? Surrounded by all this sexual addiction, are they able to go against the flow and actually build sexual integrity? Although we cannot truly gauge the secrets of the heart, we know that the outward signs indicate that we too are losing ground. Most Christian men under the age of 20 masturbate regularly,[6] and a majority of Christian men bring into marriage a regular habit of masturbation.[7] Sixty percent of married Christian men fantasize about having sex with women other than their spouse.[8] One in four Christian married men actually engage in an adulterous affair.[9] Let me repeat, one-fourth of married Christian men are acting upon their sexual fantasies through physical affairs!

How do you fit into the picture? Are you like the majority of single men who partake in premarital sex? Are you one of the one in four married men having an affair? Perhaps you're content to be one of the countless men who are engaging in sexual affairs of the mind through pornography or illicit fantasy?

Even if you're in the tiny portion of men not defined by these type of statistics, what have you done to reach out a hand to all those around you who are too afraid to ask for help? Without a true form of *networking partner,* most men will remain a statistic, a benchwarmer. Besides, this book is still as much for you because it guides you in living out a Proven life across the board.

It's so easy to justify sexual impurity in an era of the way the American media culture glorifies sex, making almost nothing off limits or taboo. Christian men are bombarded daily with sexuality. Unfortunately, about the only place where the topic of sex is off limits is in the church; therefore, most Christian men are left to fend for themselves. The results are predictable. Christian men too are losing the battle for purity.

Protectors, Not Predators

I received a telephone call from Pastor Bob who was asked by his church board to take a sabbatical after confessing that he visited a pornography website. Like the rest of us, Bob's problem didn't just happen overnight. Without telling anyone, he was facing the fact that his wife had been sleeping in a separate room for months because they lacked any real intimacy. Mounting pressures from work and an unstable home front had cracked his spiritual armor long before he made a few too many clicks on his computer. Bob didn't realize the danger until he found himself staring at a woman from his church as she bent over and the outline of her underwear could be seen through her slacks. When he started wondering about the color of her underwear, the old feelings crept over him. He knew he needed help. While recounting this story to me, with tears and a trembling voice, Bob cried, "As a pastor, I am supposed to be a protector, not a predator."

Those words are haunting. It's the same for us. Proven Men are supposed to be protectors, not predators. Apostle Paul wrote two letters to his young friend Timothy. In them, Paul provided vivid examples of both types of men, predators and protectors. Essentially, Paul said,

> *PREDATORS search out weak-willed women and view them as objects of desire.*[10]

> *PROTECTORS treat young women as sisters and view them with absolute purity.*[11]

Paul warned Timothy to have nothing to do with predators, because they are selfish, ungrateful, proud, lovers of money, and conceited. On the outside, they have an appearance of being Godly, but inside they love pleasure instead of God. They pose as Christians in order to wiggle their way into the lives of naive women, but only to satisfy their own selfish desires.[12]

It's scary how easy it is to go through the motions of being a Godly man while thinking like a predator. That used to be the only way I thought. Maybe it was looking lustfully at a waitress or undressing another man's wife with my eyes. The point is, any time we treat a woman as an object of lust, we've crossed over. Each time we take a second look, click on a pornographic image, or drift into illicit fantasy, we are acting like predators.

Paul encouraged Timothy to act as a protector instead—to all people. With older men, he was to respect and honor them as he would his own father. For younger men, he was to guide them as you would a beloved brother. Regarding older women, he was to treat them as though they were his own mother. And finally, as to young women, he was to think of them as sisters and behave with absolute purity.[13]

Nobody wants to be a predator posing as a protector—the type of man Paul warned Timothy against—who never give over completely to God's knowledge of the truth.[14] Don't be fooled. You cannot play with fire and escape getting burned.

Unlike Timothy, Bob flirted with temptation before falling. But it taught him an invaluable lesson. Today, he constantly reminds himself that he is "a protector, not a predator." Bob is finally living a Proven life.

You too are in a spiritual battle against the forces of evil. The good news is that you're called to be a knight, not a raider. As one of His agents, the King of the Universe has entrusted you with His spiritual weapons to protect. So plan to be a blessing to others instead of looking for ways to use them. It may be difficult at first, but instead of lusting after women, pray for them. After all, you're commanded by the Lord to think of women as sisters and train your eyes to treat them with absolute purity.[15]

In Bondage to Impurity

There are many reasons why men remain trapped in bondage to sexual sin. Freedom, however, begins by recognizing the nature of your sinful state. Unless you accept your need for change, it won't last. Keep an open heart and be ready to respond as you continue reading this book.

It's time to stop playing games with purity. We must purpose to overcome sexual immorality.[16] Consider a few common sexual sins and how they interfere with your relationships.

Lustful thoughts are real sins. Perhaps they are the most overlooked and yet dangerous type of sexual sin. Because they are hidden, lustful thoughts don't receive much attention.

Sexual fantasies are fabricated scenarios intended to serve you, please you, and give you what you think you deserve. In fact, some men don't consider sexual thoughts to be wrong, as long as they aren't acted upon physically. Jesus says, however, that anyone who even looks at a woman lustfully commits adultery in his heart.[17]

Why are lustful thoughts so serious that God calls them "adultery"?

The Lord desires your heart, plain and simple. Jesus doesn't want from you mere outward appearances or outward actions.[18] It's your inward thinking that reveals the true focus of your heart.

You cannot serve two masters at the same time.[19] This means you can't fuel selfish sexual desires while seeking to love and serve the Lord. You may try, but you'll always be frustrated in the end.

Sexual fantasies are forms of *false intimacy*[20] that keep you from being fully devoted to real relationships that are open and honest. Fantasies tend to make you view people as objects. Lustful thoughts can also demonstrate that you're not content.[21] When you're not content it's because some area of your life is not in line with God.

When you lust, you're seeking more and more self pleasures in a vain attempt to try to fill a void in your life. You incorrectly think that if you only had more sexual pleasures, you would be fulfilled. But this type of lust can never satisfy and it doesn't fill the place in your heart meant for Jesus. The result is emptiness because you're pushing aside real intimate relationships with the Lord and with others. By remaining pure in your thought life, you also avoid feelings of guilt and shame that only drive you further in the destructive cycle of seeking temporary pleasure of a momentary fantasy that leaves you feeling empty or deficient.

My SAD Diagnosis

Everyone knows someone who has Attention Deficit Disorder. I didn't have ADD, but SAD. My lustful thought life was a purposeful product of my Sexual Active Daydreams—my very SAD thought life.

My subconscious mind was given free reign to capture sexual images throughout the day. It was like I hired a professional photographer with a camera inside my eyes. Whenever I entered a room, I would scan it looking for every woman who might make a good actress for my fantasy film to be played in my mind. My eyes would go up and down, all around, positioning the camera for a view. Every woman was stared at, leered at, and compared. They were all simply objects for my hungering lust.

Although my heart was constantly in lust mode, I didn't necessarily daydream of having sex on the spot. My practice was to store up images for later. In doing so, I didn't want to overlook anyone.

In that sense, I treated every woman as an object and potential fantasy. When there was a pretty woman that might make a good candidate for my permanent storage files, I could almost hear in my head, "click, click, click, zoom in, click, click, click." All of these images were stored until nighttime when the pictures would be organized and I would pick and choose which images to use in fantasy as I created sexual scenes in my mind borrowing the image of the top models of the day. That was my daily ritual and it always culminated in masturbation just before going to sleep.

Any pattern of lust is very destructive. It leads to viewing women as objects. It keeps you from being open. It keeps you in slavery to a secret world.

Pornography is an advanced form of lust. Pornography stimulates fantasies and lustful thoughts and involves a heightened and direct inward focus on the satisfying of your personal desires. Although you often try to self justify it with notions that you deserve a little pleasure or that nobody gets hurt, you and others are damaged.[22] For instance, pornography breeds discontentment and fills your mind with thoughts that consume your attention and distract you from pursuing what is good. Whether you admit it or not, when you look at pornography there are inside of you feelings of guilt or shame that feed a continual downward cycle. This causes you to isolate portions of your life from others and hide from God. This desensitizes and blinds you to the truth about relationships.

There is so much more that needs to be said about pornography that we devoted the entirety of Chapter 3 to addressing it.

The family also suffers when men fail to strive for sexual integrity. Can you imagine being a young woman today looking for a husband? Surely, it's frightening for her to enter into marriage when the majority of men are so unfaithful in thought and deed.

What about a wife who marries a man not knowing he is addicted to Internet pornography?

One reason pornography tears a family apart is that a wife's greatest need in marriage is *security*. She doesn't want a husband that even thinks about having sex with another woman. She needs to be the one and only woman in her husband's heart. She longs to be treasured and pursued. However, her security is broken when her husband looks lustfully at another woman, whether it's taking a second look strolling down the street or clicking on a website to find an idolized picture of a woman. She also feels neglected when a husband uses his energy elsewhere, such as escaping into fantasy or masturbation.

What's the Solution?

How can millions of men fight against the undertow of the current and live out victory? Is it possible for single men to remain pure before marriage? Can a married man remain faithful to his wife in his heart and thoughts, as well as his body? Is it possible for a married man who is addicted to sex to break free and remain free?

The good news is that God is in the business of restoration and granting victory against the odds. Regardless of your past, God is standing ready to repair the damage, restore your relationships, and bring true meaning into your life. The Lord not only has a plan and purpose for you, but right now is calling you into His service—the only place where true joy and contentment is found. The Lord offers unconditional love, not shame, to lead you to His rest. He replaces joy for anger, peace for anxiousness, and purity for lust. He is offering you His power and plan for sexual integrity. The only real answer is to discipline your sexual urges by first fixing your gaze upon the Lord, the true source of satisfaction.

It's time to see your thoughts and conduct as God does. It's time to be broken over how you have used God's gift of sexual intimacy for selfish purposes and practices. A hard or selfish heart won't hear God or seek lasting change. It's time to ask yourself, "Am I humble enough and seeking to be close enough to the Lord to be able to hear His voice in this regard?" Consider the following verse:

> *Therefore, I urge you, brothers, in view of God's mercy, to offer your bodies as living sacrifices, holy and pleasing to God—this is your spiritual act of worship. Do not conform any longer to the pattern of this world, but be transformed by the renewing of your mind. Then you will be able to test and approve what God's will is—His good, pleasing and perfect will.*[23]

To begin living out God's will for you requires turning to the Lord with a willing heart and teachable spirit. You must ask God to speak to you and to reveal what areas of life you're holding onto control, instead of yielding to Him. Then, as you begin evaluating your own actions and motives, you keep asking yourself questions such as:

- *Is it my desire to be a living offering to a holy God?*
- *Am I able to discern God's will for my life?*
- *Under God's scrutiny are my thoughts, motives or actions absolutely pure?*
- *Am I relying upon views of others or societal norms to justify my sexual practices?*

The Lord doesn't want you to remain ignorant about sin. He wants you to overcome it.

Self-Help Won't Help

Some men incorrectly think that they can fix the problem on their own. They think that sexual sins are somehow an isolated part of their lives and all will be well once they build up enough willpower to overcome it. That's not the case. Consider this Bible passage:

> *Since you died with Christ to the basic principles of this world, why, as though you still belonged to it, do you submit to its rules: 'Do not handle! Do not taste! Do not touch!'? These are all destined to perish with use, because they are based on human commands and teachings. Such regulations indeed have an appearance of wisdom, with their self-imposed worship, their false humility and their harsh treatment of the body, but they lack any value in restraining sensual indulgence.*[24]

Don't you see how rules, such as avoiding certain practices, fail to stop the desire to lust or look at pornography? This explains why making lists or setting strict boundaries about what magazines to read, movies to watch, Internet sites to visit, or stores to avoid won't free you from lust or addiction to pornography or masturbation.

The problem with all self-help techniques and efforts is that they are of human origin and will eventually crumble. Just as pornography or fantasies bring only momentary pleasure, self-effort only grants temporary relief. The weeds are never fully uprooted, and total freedom remains out of reach.

Counting the Costs

Two years ago Richard's wife caught him looking at pornography. He confessed that he had been addicted since his teens. Donna was devastated. It was such an ugly sin to her that she began withdrawing from Richard and wanted a divorce. With their marriage on the rocks, they decided to give counseling a try. She was willing to give Richard time to get his life together, provided he worked at it. Richard was willing to read books on addiction and attend weekly meetings at a church.

For a while, Richard seemed to be doing better—at least while under the watchful eye of his wife; a self-imposed accountability partner. She even put a password on the home computer and Richard had limited access to it.

Despite these restrictions, Richard's addiction overcame him and he was fired from work for looking at Internet pornography on his office computer. Richard's wife asked him to move out and get his life together. She told him that if he didn't change in six months, she would file for divorce.

Richard tried to make the most of the six months living solo in a cheap apartment. He even went to a marriage counselor. But his wife kept insisting Richard was still the same man. He constantly justified his actions and never really tried to win back his wife. Even his friends told Richard they couldn't see any real change. Richard still lacked true repentance. It wasn't long before the threatened divorce was final.

Intellectually, Richard knew that pornography was harmful, but he couldn't muster the energy to change. Richard lived his life day by day, without regard to tomorrow. He wanted to live a victorious life, but when he was under pressure, the only real relief he knew was to turn to fantasy through pornography. He wasn't thinking about consequences or even Bible passages with warnings such as: "You may be sure that your sin will find you out"[25] or "Can a man scoop fire into his lap without his clothes being burned?"[26]

Freedom from the bondage of sexual sin doesn't come easily. In fact, it demands everything. It's about becoming a needy, dependent servant of the Lord.

It shouldn't be so shocking to learn that a man must go all-in for Christ to gain the grace and power to lead a victorious life. Jesus made it clear what it costs to follow Him when He bluntly said, "Whoever does not carry their cross and follow me cannot be my disciple."[27] After saying these hard words, the Lord didn't back away to soft sell the price, but gave this parable about counting the costs:

> *Suppose one of you wants to build a tower. Won't you first sit down and estimate the cost to see if you have enough money to complete it? For if you lay the foundation and are not able to finish it, everyone who sees it will ridicule you, saying, 'This person began to build and wasn't able to finish.'*[28]

Christ further added, "In the same way, those of you who do not give up everything you have cannot be my disciples."[29]

Make no mistake; the cost of being a disciple of Christ is high. It means giving up everything while simultaneously yielding completely to Jesus. It's not the easy road.

Yet the cost of holding on to secret sin is even higher.

Richard didn't count the costs. He never went all-in for Christ. He only gave lip service to being a disciple. He also failed to count the costs of his sin. If Richard had made a list of everything he would lose, there's no way Richard would have decided that pornography was worth more than his job, his wife and everything else.

Most men are like Richard. They don't count the costs of sin. They never sit down and actually make a list of everything pornography or an affair would cost them. They're too busy trying to sneak a bit of pleasure from a forbidden fruit to examine it to find out if it's poison.

On the other hand, consider a man who counted the costs. As a high school teacher, Mark sees girls in low cut shirts bending over and flirting to get attention every day. Mark knew that tempting thoughts crossed through his mind, so he sat down to make a list of everything he would lose if he allowed his mind to dwell on lustful thoughts. His list included losing his loyal wife and his children. As he listed his wife's name, he could envision the tears streaming down her face if he were to start an affair with one of these girls. He knew she would be shocked and burn with anger if he even entertained a fantasy about having sex with a teen, let alone acting it out.

Before long, Mark's list filled an entire page. The price in his case would go past losing his family; it would involve wearing striped clothes and being listed on a national sex offender list requiring him to register his address every time he moved.

Mark then made a list of what he would gain if he avoided and battled the temptation. The short list of a few minutes of temporary pleasure paled in comparison to the costs. Counting the costs helped Mark choose to be on guard and to become fiercely devoted to his wife and children, which lessen the tug of the false forms of intimacy offered by fantasy or an affair.

Mark knew that making this list wouldn't keep him from being tempted, but it began the process of being resolved not to give an inch. Fantasy was not an option and he was willing to do whatever it took to remain pure in his thought life. Mark began making game plans for tempting situations. For instance, he would never be alone with a female student or any woman other than his wife.

Mark wasn't a fool. He also knew that he couldn't build the tower alone. He needed the Lord and other Proven Men. Fortunately, he found us. Today, he maintains a true *network partner* and strong community support with other Proven Men.

Examples of Joel, Tim, and Stan

Throughout the book, we will follow even more closely the stories of three particular men—Joel (myself), Tim, and Stan—as they struggle to lead lives of sexual integrity. Our stories illustrate clearly how the principles from each chapter play out in real life.

For different reasons, each of us turned to the false promise of pornography and fantasy. None of us, however, found lasting love, joy, or ecstasy. In order to succeed, each one would have to surrender to the Lord and follow God's path for purity and peace through the Proven Path.

It is our hope that the pain of our struggles will offer you a better understanding of how to apply—and not to apply—the Proven Path in your own life.

First, each man's situation will be explained here, and then you will hear more about their victories, as well as their setbacks, throughout this book. (If you would like to read each man's story as a whole, you'll find them in their entirety in Appendix E.)

▶ **JOEL: The Overachiever with Only One Thing He Couldn't Overcome**

I was a typical overachiever. My parents told me I could do or be anything I wanted and I believed it. Everything I put my mind to, I accomplished. In grade school, I was the teacher's pet and regularly praised for early accomplishments. As captain of the track team, I added acclaim in sports to good grades in high school. College and law school exams presented no obstacle; I graduated in the top 5 in my law school class. In one summer, I aced the Bar exam, married the homecoming queen, and landed a prestigious job. I regularly received bonuses and awards for accomplishments.

Yet there is one thing I couldn't overcome. I was addicted to lust and masturbation. There was much more going on than my looking at porn or lusting after women. There was an ever-present inner tension between my duality, as I desperately sought to compartmentalize my competing secret life from my public one. It was hard to bring my two worlds together. On the outside, I had a clean cup; on the inside, filth. To compensate, I made my outside appearance the cleanest in the land. Yet, guilt and shame never vanished. At times it was overwhelming. Will my secret life prevail or will my entire world crash around me?

▶ TIM: The Underachiever Who Shied Away from Real Relationships

"You're so stupid. I don't think you have the brains you were born with!" These were hard words. It was especially devastating because they came from his father, a man he looked up to. Harsh words and disappointment were the norm in Tim's life. His father made a point of telling him, "You're no good. You'll never amount to anything." Tim tried to dismiss his father, but in his heart he couldn't help but believe these assessments of himself. Actually, the inability to please his father shattered Tim's very soul. It produced intense shame, guilt and self-condemnation. "I must be defective. I don't deserve his love. I don't deserve anyone's love," Tim told himself.

Add to this the extreme guilt and shame over masturbation and you have a train wreck waiting to happen. As a child, Tim once stumbled upon a box of pornography in his uncle's work shed. It was like manna from heaven, providing a way of experiencing the human love and respect that he so desperately longed to enjoy. Will he be able to give up this one consolation and turn to God?

▶ STAN: Single and Sliding Down a Slippery Slope

Stan grew up in the church where his dad was the pastor. He attended a Christian college with the dream of making it in the music industry. He was well acquainted with Scriptures. College life was fun and he had lots of friends. Stan had time to play sports and attend parties. That's where he met Missy. Stan was nuts about her. Missy was so awesome and passionate for the Lord. She was definitely the one he planned to marry. In fact, he couldn't keep his hands off her. Their dates always turn steamy.

That's when Stan's two worlds began to collide and he knew he needed sexual integrity. His habit of masturbating to Internet porn suddenly caught up with him. All he can think about is making love with Missy. Will he be able to turn his thoughts away from sex to keep the girl of his dreams?

Chapter 2

Sexual Impurity

Ten years ago I naively drafted and actually sent to dozens of my friends a "Sexual Addiction Test" I created. My goal was to promote the idea of purity. What I got, however, was an earful from virtually everyone. Some were angry at the thought that I felt they needed to take such a test. Others took the test and rejoiced over the notion they were in the clear on purity and need not try any harder. Pastor Steve, to whom I also sent the test, wisely told me to contact each man and ask for forgiveness for sending it out. Needless to say, my test didn't accomplish my goal of leading men to become PROVEN in the area of sexual integrity.

In the years since, I have come to realize that there's no simple test to determine if a person is or isn't a sex addict. In fact, there's no consensus on a definition or even whether it should be considered a clinical condition. For instance, the American Psychiatric Association doesn't recognize sexual addiction as a diagnosis.[30] Those who do classify sexual addiction as a disorder vary greatly regarding its definition. One list cites ten requirements, beginning with a recurring failure to resist impulses to engage in extreme acts of lewd sex.[31] Others list characteristics and suggest that a person is an addict if he demonstrates a certain number of them. All attempts to define sexual addiction are fraught with vagueness and over-generalization.

One of the best books I've seen that addresses sexual addiction from a Christian perspective is *False Intimacy: Understanding the Struggle of Sexual Addiction* by Dr. Harry Schaumburg.[32] Consider these passages:

> *… at its core, sexual fantasy is a worship of self, a devotion to the ability of people to fabricate in their minds the solution to what they know is a need and believe they deserve.*

> *Sex addicts think and plan their lives around sex…. A sexually addicted person becomes fully absorbed with sex, for it becomes the greatest need—not the greatest desire. Sex is wanted, demanded, and will be pursued at any cost.*

> *The truth is, however, that when we try to bury the core reality of emptiness, the result is false intimacy, not genuine. When we insist that our needs for intimacy be fulfilled and ignore the reality that loneliness is always present, we get the very opposite of what we're demanding: We're left alone to stare with open eyes at the harsh reality of nakedness.*

Regardless of whether or not you might classify yourself as a sex addict, if you look at pornography, engage in premarital sex or marital affairs, hang out in Internet chat rooms, or even entertain fantasies throughout the day there's a strong likelihood that you are engaging in a form of false intimacy that's damaging to your relationships with God and others, including your spouse or future spouse if you're single.

Is Sex an Idol?

Is it really necessary to create a definition or peg a person as a sex addict? For most of us, and for the purposes of this book, the answer is no. But anything you turn into an idol or has mastery over you needs to be addressed.[33] You shouldn't wait until you're enslaved by it. Whenever you chase after selfish pleasure, you build a dividing wall between you and God. It's no wonder your life gets tossed upside down when sex becomes the center focus or an idol.

Sex can easily become an idol in your life if it becomes your master or a focal point of your life. Although it's difficult to become self aware, you must examine whether you're allowing some form of sex to block your perfect union with God. Here are just a few warning signs:

> *You must put on blinders to God in order to engage in it,*
> *You chase after it daily, or*
> *You feel guilty afterward.*

However, don't push aside your need to do business with sexual sin thinking you're safe as long as you haven't classified it as an addiction. If it's sinful, it must be uprooted.

Daily Duty

A misunderstood area of sexuality is the notion that a man must have sex almost every day to be satisfied. Although God purposefully designed and created you and me to be sexual beings and we certainly are capable of wanting or enjoying sex daily, God never intended that you would satisfy every desire the moment it enters your mind.[34] When you train yourself to sexualize everything, you end up wanting sex daily and lose sensitivity to real intimacy.[35] Demanding sex daily frequently can reveal that sex controls you. Sex is your master, rather than the Lord.

I used to try to convince my wife to have sex daily. I tried to justify it by saying, "God made me more sensual than other men." I now see how the man who seeks to satisfy all of his personal desires, often without true regard of his wife, is one who'll never find contentment. It never worked for me. The endless hunt for satisfaction, with sex often the target, was a constant cycle of frustration.

Sex was never enough for me, even if I could get it daily. It would not satisfy the raging fire developed by my secret thought life. I was selfishly demanding that my wife try to extinguish the flames I ignited from outside sources.

Of course, having sex daily as newlyweds is fairly common. When both spouses are on the same page, sex is a wonderful gift. However, many men race ahead of their wives in the area of sex. They don't allow their wives to honestly communicate with them regarding sex. If more husbands were to ask their wives, they may find that many wives feel pressure to have sex daily. When you have expectations about how often you should have sex, chances are you're living for self-gratification, which only sets your heart on a continuous pursuit to satisfy a desire that will always want and demand more.

Consider Greg. He didn't feel satisfied if he didn't have sex daily. Sex was how he felt loved. This put constant pressure on his wife to prove her love daily through sex, regardless of how hard her day had been or whether she was tired. Every night as she turned to go to sleep, he would make his move. Greg incorrectly felt that if they had sex daily, his marriage would be perfect. In fact, just the opposite occurred.

Because he had not established an open dialogue with his wife about sex, Greg assumed that she would consider daily sex ideal, too. This left her no room for saying she preferred having sex less often. Eventually, she filed for divorce. Greg was left not knowing whether she had been put off by his desire for daily sex or if he neglected her in other ways. Maybe she didn't like him taking it for granted that they'd have sex every night in exactly the same way. Maybe Greg was selfish in other ways, too. She may have been happy to have sex nearly every day if he had been more engaging, but he never found out because he assumed her needs were the same as his own—and he didn't ask.

Len made a similar mistake. "Physical touch cues" were Len's method of operation. Len only touched or caressed his wife as a prelude to sex. To him, it was "touch, sex." There was always a comma after he touched his wife. It was always a prelude to sex. Len didn't understand that his wife needed affectionate touching to feel a connection with him. Casual hugs, kisses and touching without an ulterior motive weren't in his repertoire. Len incorrectly thought if she engaged in any of these, it was a cue that she wanted sex. To Len, "romance" was just another word for sex. He didn't take her needs into account. He never rubbed his wife's feet just to make her feel good. For Len, all touching led to sex. It was always touch "comma" then sex. Over time, Len's wife felt manipulated and didn't even want to be touched. She couldn't simply enjoy a touch or kiss because there was always an expectation attached.

Only after striving to live a Proven life did Len begin practicing touch for its own sake, or "touch period." He made a point of giving his wife backrubs and foot massages without having sex that night. His sex life ultimately improved because his wife was no longer second fiddle to his need for sex. She felt more like a person who mattered to him and less like a sex object.

By focusing on sex or having expectations regarding how often a man must have sex, you end up training yourself to sexualize things. For instance, "double takes" blossom into rating women, which leads to wondering what they look like naked, and then thinking about what it would be like to have sex with them. This leads to more sexual fantasies. Ultimately you may even imagine having sex with them while masturbating or having sex with your wife.

The Need for Control

What causes men to be blinded by or to chase after sex? One reason people turn to pornography, masturbation, or other sexual escape is that they want to control their lives. They rely upon a chosen form of sexual activity to avoid the pain of open, vulnerable relationships. While you cannot fully control others or cause them to love you, you can control your fantasies, the person in the picture, and your own sexual body.

The truth is you do control how much of your life you open to others. For instance, you can have sex with someone but not allow them to know your spirit. People dominated by sex spend so much time in sexual fantasies that they run from real relationships. Even when they connect with a woman in real life, they end up depersonalizing them as an object of lust. This can turn sex, which is a valid aspect of intimacy with a spouse, into an inward, self-pleasing form of phantom relationship. When that happens, even a spouse is treated as an object rather than a spiritual partner with whom to grow in deepest intimacy and vulnerability to the point of being transparent and single-minded in heart.

In our 12-week companion study named, *The 12-Week Study to a PROVEN Path to Sexual Integrity,* we say a lot more about the need for control and causes for sexual impurity. For now, in the next chapter, let's focus on some particular areas of sexual sin—including pornography, premarital sex and post-marital affairs—and even consider ways chat rooms or instant messaging can cross the line. After laying this foundation, we'll address the Proven Path for sexual integrity.

Passionate for God,
Repentant in spirit,
Open and honest,
Victorious in living,
Eternal in perspective, and
Networking with other *Proven Men.*

Chapter

Pornography

Pornography is by far the biggest money maker on the Internet. We are sexual beings who were created for relationships. These innate needs are powerful forces that can create cravings as strong as hunger for food.

People spend billions of dollars a year to buy Internet porn because it does not and cannot supply the real needs that are missing in life. In other words, people keep trying to force it to work by buying more and more. Many websites offer free sneak previews or thumbnail pictures because they know that people won't be satisfied and will only crave greater thrills. Eventually, some turn to harder core and more costly pictures in the vain hope that these more expensive fantasies will satisfy.

Porn promises a form of sex that doesn't require any effort. The woman in the picture smiles brightly. She demands nothing, but wants to provide everything you can imagine. She's always available at your convenience and requires no further commitment.

With pornography you're in control of your fantasies, the person in the picture, and your own sexual body. Pornography appears to be the perfect partner. When combined with mastur-bation, pornography masquerades as a convenient substitute for sex with a real person.

The problem is pornography only provides a sexual release. It doesn't satisfy any emotional needs, but leaves you feeling empty or guilty. It can lead to becoming compulsive about using porn for the high of sexual release and keep increasing the activity in a vain attempt at trying to force pornography to work as a substitute for true intimacy. Many eventually spend hours a day viewing Internet pornography. Others masturbate up to ten times a day. They remain on a constant hunt for more, newer, and better ways to feed the desire for a moment of pleasure while also hoping that the vacuum in their soul is filled. Although they may receive temporary relief from the issues of the world they are trying to escape from, they're ultimately left feeling empty. Guilt and shame lurk beneath the surface. Instead of feeling in control, as they did initially, they feel completely out of control, at the mercy of their addiction. They often lack any real sense of contentment and purpose. In the end, this double life creates loneliness because they don't let others in. The addiction has them in its grip.

Pornography Harms Real Relationships

Pornography actually damages your real relationships with God and others. This is because illicit lust and fanciful expecta-tions are self-centered and anti-relational. Over time you end up training yourself to be selfishly served and instantly gratified. You also discipline yourself to withhold love and feelings. A self-centered effort to control life and the effort of relationships ends up blocking your perfect union with God. When you chase after the idols of selfish pleasure, you build a dividing wall. Each time you turn to pornography, you must put on blinders to the Lord (and your spouse, if you're married).

By walking in step with the world, you turn away from the One who created you and loves you most. You stop listening to God's voice and cannot discern His will. Even your prayer requests of God often go unanswered because they're selfish.[36] You end up drifting through life self-deceived; thinking that your ways can bring satisfaction.

It's the sin of trying to live independently from God that makes chasing after sexual pleasures of pornography wrong. God purposely created both male and female to unite in sexual pleasure as husband and wife, yet those who chase after the false allure of pornography have closed their eyes to the Lord and are seeking to create their own universe. That's the essence of why men remain trapped in bondage to pornography. They have pridefully turned away and closed out God.

You also damage your relationship with a spouse (or your future spouse, if you're single) by depersonalizing women. Repeatedly turning to pornography and fantasy causes you to view women as sex objects. Think about it. You always look at women naked. You stare and lust after hundreds, even thousands, of women, all of whom are naked. Their sole purpose is to provide you with sex. Thus, sex becomes an inward, self-pleasing form of phantom relationship. Women become nothing more than objects of your sexual desire.

It's also inevitable that you'll compare your real spouse with the airbrushed perfect naked image in the pornographic images you have sex with the most. What real person could ever measure up to that fantasy? Looking at pornography, including reading sex forums or stories, creates false ideas of what sex is like and how it should take place. They then demand a perfect body. They demand sexual pleasure focused on themselves.

Pornography can also create a barrier to healthy sex. Because of their guilt about pornography, some men may start to think of sex itself as sinful. This could carry over to their sexual life with their wife. If they find some aspects of sex dirty or off limits, their inhibitions may leave them unable to perform sexually.

This is exactly what happened to Jack. He was addicted to pornography and he knew it. When he was 12, he looked at his first hard-core porn magazine. He felt that looking at a woman's private parts in a magazine was evil, but he kept staring and masturbating. The guilt carried forward into marriage, where he was not comfortable looking at his wife's naked body. He felt that sex was dirty and needed to be done in secret. Therefore, he couldn't give up pornography even years into marriage, and he couldn't be truly intimate with his wife.

Ben had a similar problem. He masturbated nearly a dozen times a day prior to getting married. Ben was constantly filled with shame and guilt. Feelings of inadequacy and the habit of masturbation both carried over into his marriage. The emotional scars produced from years of objectifying women and hiding in fantasy even prevented Ben from being able to obtain a normal erection during intimacy with his wife.

Despite what you might think, a husband's real sex life with his real wife suffers when he has porn-driven sex. When you turn to pornography, you're being lazy regarding sex. You don't want to put in the effort to relate to your own wife. You prefer the "sex slave" in your fantasy.

Trust me—your wife will know if you're looking at pornography by the way you treat her. She may not know you are turning to porn, but a wife knows when her husband is distracted or gives his attention elsewhere—to another, even when the mistress is an idolized picture.

Right after I confessed my addiction to my wife, she told me she had known all along that I was masturbating. We actually both sheepishly chuckled when she told me that she had not been asleep all those nights I had masturbated. I didn't fool her. But sadly, she somehow thought that if she were just prettier or better in bed I would stop. It ended any hint of humor as I recounted all the hours I had spent devoting myself to fantasies of other women at her expense.

A lot of women feel the same way. Just because they're not saying anything to you, it doesn't mean they don't feel it. One day, our friend Jill called my wife crying. She said her husband didn't love her anymore. He didn't make her feel cherished. He didn't pursue her. He was distant and distracted. After the crying ended, Jill asked my wife how to find out if her husband was looking at pornography.

What happens when a wife discovers the truth? Most women are repulsed at the thought that their husbands have been looking at pornography and fantasizing about other women. Trust and respect are shattered. Most are terrified that they're being measured against another woman, a model, or worse yet, a fantasy they know they can never match. When a woman doesn't feel cherished, she withdraws emotionally and sexually. Some women eventually seek divorce, considering pornography to be a sexual sin equivalent to adultery—something they cannot compete with.

In truth, those turning to pornography generally are treating women, including their spouse, as an object of pleasure rather than a partner. Yes, if you turn to porn, you're treating women—you're treating your wife—as a sex object. That will surely damage your relationship.

Pornography Fuels Anger

Two of the biggest struggles men face today are pornography and anger. What you may not know is that pornography fuels anger. They go hand-in-hand. Anger is the outpouring of energy in response to a goal that's blocked. You get frustrated when your needs or expectations aren't met, and express your frustration in anger.[37] When this happens, you end up pushing others away (including the Lord). Pornography breeds this frustration.

At its core, pornography is a form of false intimacy. It substitutes sex for real intimacy. Pornography replaces reality with fantasies that can never materialize. Since no real woman can duplicate your pornographic fantasy world, real relationships disappoint and frustrate.

Pornography also centers upon escaping into fantasy. It's a hideaway, a place where you're always in complete control. However, no matter how hard you try, you cannot control life, circumstances, and others. When you realize that the expectation created by your fantasy cannot be met, it can provoke anger deep within of you.

Pornography can also create anger by leading you to isolate yourself. You build up walls to avoid the criticism, pain, sadness, or other undesirable emotions that go along with real relationships. You also withhold yourself (and love or kindness) from others, as you train yourself to be the only one served. Yet, loneliness breeds anger.

When you display anger, you reveal that you don't really believe that God is good or that you can trust Him with your life. Stated another way, you're attempting to run your own life—caring more about your circumstances and rights than about seeking the Lord and enjoying Him.

However, self-seekers will always remain trapped in bondage to some form of sin, whether it be pornography, sexual impurity, greed, bitterness, or anger. They will constantly feel the weight of frustration. They will be angry. Consider this passage:

> *But for those who are self-seeking and who reject the truth and follow evil, there will be wrath and anger. There will be trouble and distress for every human being who does evil.*[38]

Did you know that one common reaction to internal anger (and to the things that lead to anger) is drifting into fantasy? This escape mechanism takes many forms, such as dreaming of revenge, fantasizing about being a hero, or dwelling upon sexual activities. Perhaps you never realized just how much anger leads you to turn to pornography. It's the perfect escape. It's also a vicious downward spiral where you bounce back and forth between anger and escaping to porn.

Each time Josh has a fight with his wife he says to himself, "Who needs her!" He storms out of the house and drives away. But where can he go? Usually he ends up at the local store that sells pornography. There, he drifts into fantasy. He stares intently at the women looking lustfully back at him. He imagines that these women see his perfection and long to meet his every need. This is what he deserves. Beneath the surface anger resides, although for now temporarily soothed through a momentary escape. However, when he returns home, his real wife isn't so accommodating. She remains angry over the fight and doesn't see having sex as the way to make up. Josh tunes her out, thinking, "If only she could be like the woman on the magazine cover."

George hates his demeaning job and he barely makes enough to pay the bills. When he gets home, George is physically exhausted because his job requires a lot of lifting. He longs to be greeted at the door with hugs and kisses, to feel like the king of at least his one-bedroom castle. However, his wife is always distracted. It just seems like too much effort to keep asking for attention or affection. Although it doesn't flare up into huge fights, George is angry with his lot in life. Therefore, George frequently heads straight to the bathroom to look at his hidden magazine, where he can dream of a different life. It won't be long before he has to return to reality. He just doesn't have the energy to reach out to his wife, so he stays up late watching TV or looking at Internet pornography.

In short, anger is the companion of sexual impurity—in particular, pornography. Not only does pornography breed anger, but anger feeds the desire to escape into the fantasy world of pornography. Together, they drag you ever further away from healthy, real relationships.

In some ways, I felt my wife was a ball and chain around my leg. She held me back from doing what I wanted. Whenever she would go away for a short time I shouted, "I am free. Free to do whatever I want." The "whatever" always was sexual fantasy and masturbation. It was one thing in life that never seemed to demand, but always wanted to give. Yet, it was a mirage.

Explaining his relationship with his wife, Brian once related to me a story of how one day while they were walking in the woods together, his wife ran away screaming. I asked why. According to Brian, she had no reason. He did finally reveal that his wife said she was afraid of him. I asked if he had been angry. He denied it, but did admit that he had broken a stick.

"How big was the stick?" I asked. Apparently, it was a walking stick about three inches in diameter. With a few more questions, Brian finally came to realize that he must have hit the stick pretty hard to break it. It took a bit longer for him to accept that he had been angry after all.

The root issue might stem from being recently treated unfairly or suffering some form of abuse as a child. The list of reasons or contributing factors to anger may be quite long and varied, but the results are the same: a hidden fear of being vulnerable, that creates a heightened desire for control and fear of intimacy.

Why Are Men Stuck?

The biggest reason men are stuck is that most men don't really want to stop escaping through pornography. They don't hate porn or masturbation, but simply want the guilt and shame to stop.

Let's be real. Pornography does feel good at the moment. Looking at a beautiful woman is appealing. Pornography is also a welcome escape device when a man is bored or if someone treats him harshly or unfairly. When you add masturbation to the mix, it's downright as addicting as many drugs.

But how can a man turn away from a behavior that can feel good? The good news is that victory is not based upon being repulsed by pornography. Rather, as explained later, seeing pornography as unwelcome involves a decision to die to selfishness. It's a decision to accept God's design for intimacy and to steer clear of false forms of intimacy.

I would lie if I were to say that I'm still not tempted to take escape into sexual fantasy. It would also be false to pretend that my eyes would burn if pornography was set before me. I don't find these things repulsive. That's not what is meant by hating pornography. Rather, I have chosen to reject lustful thoughts. I have chosen to hate leaving God for an empty promise of a short temporary pleasure. Therefore, I choose not to look at pornography. In that sense, I hate pornography. Nevertheless, my battle is not one day at a time, but one thought at a time. I wake up each morning with a resolve to be on guard. I cannot become complacent.

I must purpose to take captive *every* thought and conform it to Christ.[39] Each time I fail, I return to God by following the model and practices addressed in this book.

This is the type of resolve needed to overcome pornography. It also requires that you ask God to reveal to you the evil of pornography and to cause you to hate it because it blocks you from enjoying the Lord. Purpose to hate it also for the harm it causes others. Each time you use pornography, it leads someone else into sin.[40] You're the market that lures others to exchange their self-respect for money or attention. You indirectly cause them to blind their eyes from seeing God as they uncover their bodies for the insatiable lust of others. Innocence is taken from those who want to be desired and loved when they trade it away for a lie. Even their so-called consent doesn't justify your participation in what kills their souls and leads them into an ever-degrading path of destruction.

Hating pornography isn't easy. When Kevin first confessed to his wife that he was regularly looking at pornography, she could see that he wasn't fully repentant over the sin. She calmly stated, "You're only sorry you got caught." Kevin wanted to lash out at her, but she was right. He still didn't hate his sin. Sure, he didn't like the shame and guilt afterward, but Kevin had to admit that he secretly enjoyed the moment. Kevin needed to retrain his thinking and living. From then on, he kept focusing on how sin grieved God, and how he didn't want to grieve God any longer. Kevin kept reminding himself: "Pornography is sin, and God hates sin; therefore, I hate sin." He continually went to the Lord and placed himself in a position to receive true repentance in order to want to turn from pornography and any other things he placed ahead of his relationships with the Lord and his wife.

When Bruce first gave up pornography, he couldn't go to the mailbox to pick up the mail because his heart would race if he would even see the cover of certain magazines. Bruce was not a freak. All men are wired visually. Actually Bruce was wise not to play with fire and to ask his wife to pick up the mail. She knew not to leave any magazine on the countertop that even had a picture of a woman on the cover. Bruce needed time to recondition his mind as he set out to hate pornography.

Until you see pornography and its accompanying lust and fantasy as wrong because it damages relationships, you'll only pretend to stop. Even if you must ask God every day for weeks, don't stop petitioning the Lord in earnest for a heart that hates chasing after pornography.

Are you a bit anxious about whether you really can give up pornography? Good. The truth is you can't do this in your own strength. You'll face many challenges and you have years of backward thinking to undo and old habits to break and replace. Although not a program or list of steps to follow, there is a Proven Path for victory over pornography, which is explained in Part II.

BE ON GUARD.

Passionate for God,
Repentant in spirit,
Open and honest,
Victorious in living,
Eternal in perspective, and
Networking with other *Proven Men.*

Chapter

Affairs: Pre-Marital and Post-Marital

n affair is any emotional or sexual relationship, regardless of how brief, between two people who are not married to each other. Next to pornography, an affair might just be the biggest form of sexual impurity affecting men. Most single men buy into the lie that premarital sex is all right. But it's no less an affair than adultery and carries with it deep scars into marriage. Married men don't fare much better. Most are ensnared by post-marital affairs, whether emotional or physical, which soils their marriage. Because affairs are often emotional before turning sexual, chat rooms (and even instant messaging) are an often-overlooked breeding ground for affairs.

Premarital Affairs

What's the big deal about premarital sex? After all, everyone is doing it. Besides, aren't both people consenting adults?

It's easy to dispatch the first justification, namely that it is okay today because most young people sleep together before getting

43

married. The folly is revealed as you realize that the same is true about everyone gossiping, being selfish or proud, and envious.[41] We know better. Just because others do something doesn't make it right. Yet somehow we wonder if premarital sex is some sort of exception. Well, I doubt it's a coincidence that the Bible uses sexual impurity over and over again as a backdrop for explaining that we should not conform to the pattern of this world. We've already read where the Bible spells out that we should offer our bodies as living sacrifices as a spiritual act of worship, and to do so we must no longer conform to ways of the world.[42] The Bible adds to this insight by reminding you that the only way you can stop chasing after the sinful desires of the flesh is by living under control by the Holy Spirit.[43] The point is made with force by telling you to actually put to death whatever belongs to your earthly nature, such as sexual immorality, impurity, and lust.[44]

In short, you're told to go against the norm of society's sex-based worldview as a way of praising God as well as protecting your marriage.

What does the world say? During high school, "sexual education" teaches teens to begin experimenting with sex. Nearly one-half of all high school students comply and are having sexual intercourse.[45] By the time of marriage, only a few remain a virgin.

What most singles pin their hope upon is the justification, "No one is hurt" or "She consented, so where is the harm?" Well, allow me to ask a question: Would you invite your girlfriend to rob a bank with you? Not likely. You understand that she'll be equally guilty of a crime. Her consent won't clear you from the consequences if you get caught. The fact that both of you consent to premarital sex is no different.

Isn't the correct approach to settle whether premarital sex violates God's design for you (and your future wife)? God perfectly

44

created male and female. A husband and wife complement each other. Marriage is a union, such a perfect fit that two become one.[46] The master design was for a couple to permanently join physically, mentally, emotionally, and spiritually. When entering into this lifelong commitment, the bride and groom make irrevocable vows that the union will never be broken, neither by divorce nor through the giving of oneself to any other. Wow. What a great design for a perfect relationship as a representation of our permanent relationship with Christ.

However, when you act outside of this union in ways such as premarital sex (or affairs or divorce), you reject God's gift in order to chase after temporary pleasure, which never really fully satisfies.

Why does God want you to wait for sex until marriage? Who better to instruct you than the One who created you and instituted marriage? Reserving sex for marriage is according to God's design. When the Lord tells you to wait, you can be sure it's not to withhold His love or gifts, and it's not some silly contest just to see if you can do it. God wants to protect you from harm. He knows that premarital sex not only endangers your body but also scars your soul and spirit.

Sexual misconduct always harms you in many ways. The easiest symptom to recognize is the ever-present feelings of guilt and shame. Of course, you'll also need to keep shutting your heart from God to keep engaging in premarital sex.

What singles often overlook is the effect of "sexual unity" caused by premarital sex. It's not only very powerful, but often clouds other issues or problems in a relationship and fools you into thinking that this woman is the one God has designed for me. Only after you marry do these incompatibility issues begin to take a heavy toll.

Not every woman is right for you. Otherwise, everyone would marry the first girl they asked on a date and we would never have any divorces. I am so glad that I did not marry any one of the girls I dated before I married my wife!

Think through some of the reasons your dating relationships or your friend's ended. Sometimes they are over big issues such as whether she wanted a career and not kids. Other times they are more subtle, such as when she never makes you feel respected or she always complains. The problem with having premarital sex is that you feel more connected because of the sex and end up overlooking these red flags or differences that would otherwise have led to breaking up.

Pre-marriage sexual unity also affects women differently. First, your future wife doesn't want you practicing sex with every girlfriend. She will feel cheated and worry about being compared.

Second, women often better understand and more deeply feel the emotional impact of sexual union. They know that it's needed to be built on mutual trust and respect. Therefore, she'll be hurt because of your premarital sex with her regardless of whether you ultimately marry her. She wants a man that treats it as sexual intimacy, not sex. Your refusal to wait shows your view.

Maybe you use the justification that you're going to get married. What's to say that you will actually get married? Nearly one-half of couples that live together don't end up getting married,[47] and those that do have a significantly higher rate of divorce,[48] so why do you think by having sex that it seals the deal? Maybe before she says "I do" she will begin to doubt that you will be a faithful husband after you marry if all you can think about is sex.

If you don't marry, you each carry into the next relationship thoughts and memories of each prior sexual encounter. This can have a devastating effect on your marriage. Not only will you compare your wife to a prior sexual encounter with someone else, but it's worth repeating that your wife will be fearful of such comparison. Trust me, it will create trust issues and affect your love life after you put on the wedding ring.

Assuming you do marry the first girl you sleep with, she will still likely blame you for not protecting her purity, which leads to respect and resentment issues in marriage. That's right. After you marry her, in all likelihood, she will regret premarital sex and it will result in guilt, shame, resentment, or anger.

Guess who is the cause of this? What's more, guess what impact this will have on your married sex life? A hurt or resentful wife will not be open to enjoying the full intimacy of sex in marriage. That's right. As hard as it may be for you to accept or believe, your sex life after you marry will be affected by premarital sex—often even more magnified than while you were having premarital sex.

Simply saying that you are sorry after the fact doesn't instantly repair her damaged spirit. It will take a lot of time and patience, and perhaps counseling, for her to open her soul (and her love making) fully.

You don't agree? Just ask a married man who didn't wait for sex whether his wife regrets it. That's right. Most women (if they are honest) regret having premarital sex after they got married. This guilt does carry over into marriage, and you're the one who did not protect her from it.

Need more convincing? Ask husbands how this guilt and shame has actually hindered their sex life now that they are married. That's right. Couples that had premarital sex are frequently less satisfied with sex after they marry.

Remember when you whispered into her ear that you'll be forever faithful to her if she agrees to have sex before marriage? The statistics show that this is faulty thinking. Men who are not willing to wait for sex in marriage are also more likely to cross that same line in marriage by having affairs. There are similar statistics for women having affairs.

Why should this be a surprise? You rejected God's purpose for sex and think it's available to all consenting adults. Of course, you doubt that you'll be unfaithful in thought or deed. But based on what? The same strength you had in waiting until marriage?

Remaining sexually pure before marriage is one of the hardest battles a single man will face. It's something that will require more strength than you have. It will test what kind of a man you want to be. Will you be Proven or selfish? Will you trust in yourself or the Lord?

Don't let premarital sex get in the way of your relationship with God and the woman of your dreams. Rather, find out what pleases the Lord. You might surprise yourself that it really is worth the wait. As you pursue real intimacy over sex you'll find that a wonderful byproduct awaits; that you actually get to know your future wife, including her hopes, dreams, and fears. You'll be her one and only knight in shining armor.

Of course, if you already crossed that line, all is not lost. You can still live out a Proven life and usher in healing and restoration into your marriage. God is in the business of restoration. Begin your renewed virginity today.

Post-Marital Affairs

Post-marital affairs are often unplanned, but quickly get out of control before either party realizes what's happening. They do a great deal of damage whether or not they progress to physical adultery.

Zach was a married man with wandering eyes. He thought he was good at hiding his lustful stares, but one day at an evening church service his eyes met Martha's. To his surprise, she didn't look away, but reciprocated his gaze. It was pretty thrilling to exchange secret glances. At subsequent church events, Zach searched for Martha. She continued to return his glances. Zach made efforts to sit next to her and her husband at church functions. As couples, they began inviting each other over for game nights. On the surface, the four grew in friendship. Below the surface, however, an emotional bond was forming between Zach and Martha. Soon, Zach and Martha began sharing secret telephone calls and instant messages on Facebook. This lasted six months and ended only when Zach's wife needed to use his computer and found the messages they wrote to each other. It took years to rebuild trust and for Zach to uncover and work through his pattern of engaging in many aspects of false intimacy.

Physical affairs aren't the only way your marriage is damaged. Often the emotional affair is the silent killer.

An emotional affair without sex typically begins either when a married man has feelings for a woman other than his wife or when he regularly looks at pornography and engages in fantasy. An emotional affair is very alluring because it's supercharged with emotion. It can have the same energy and attraction as when a man was first dating his wife. He enjoys the sound of her voice or the words she says in her emails.

Don't be complacent. It's easy for this to occur. Maybe you're mad at your wife, so you start chatting with that attractive secretary at work. You've known her for years, so it's easy. Pretty soon you're sharing intimate things about your marriage. She reciprocates by sharing her problems with her boyfriend. She loves the fact that you pay attention to her and that you think she has important things to say. She also confirms how hard you have it and says you deserve better. One day she even suggests that maybe you should leave your wife and suggests going to lunch to talk more about it.

A secret emotional affair has a magnetic pull. You find in it something you're not getting at home: a sympathetic ear of a woman who understands and deeply cares about you and your life. You're energized each time you talk with her. Even while apart, you spend time imagining what she's doing. If your wife confronts you, you insist you have done nothing wrong. After all, it's all been taking place in your mind. You've never kissed her or said "I love you."

So why is an emotional affair so deadly? It steals emotional energy from your marriage. Even though no physical boundary is crossed, you're robbing your wife of your best communication and having your emotional needs met by someone else. You may even end up saving topics of conversation for the other woman, instead of your wife, who gets the leftovers. You withhold love in many other ways too. Because you are getting some of your emotional needs met outside of marriage, you don't put 100 percent into the marriage. In the back of your mind you know there is someone else out there for you, so you don't have to work so hard at this relationship.

Because a purely emotional affair is non-sexual, it's often the hardest to recognize or recover from. First, there is no deep feeling of guilt—not the level of guilt you would feel from having a physical affair or even the guilt from masturbation. The spouse entangled in the emotional relationship may justify it as "friendship" or "innocent fun" due to the lack of physical contact. It's difficult to repent from something you don't see as sinful.

Second, there are other hidden reasons why a man hides in "safer" forms of false intimacy over the work involved in a healthy relationship with his spouse. Perhaps you're afraid your wife wouldn't love you if she knew the "real you." If so, it's safer to keep her at a distance. Or maybe it's just too much work to be transparent. It's possible that your wife always pushes aside your hopes and dreams. Maybe you simply lack the energy to become aware of your true feelings. Whatever the reason, you think true intimacy with her is not worth the effort.

A non-sexual emotional affair doesn't require 100 percent effort. It's on the margins. You can give as little or as much to it as you like and no one will ask more of you. An emotional tie to another woman doesn't require vulnerability or deep commitment. You control the space, time and energy. It's like having a mistress who gladly accepts only what you can easily provide and willingly focuses on your best attributes, while your wife takes care of your more mundane needs in life. It seems to be the best of both worlds. However, there's always a negative impact on the real marriage and upon your own heart and soul. Leading a double life always has a high price.

Collectively I was having an emotional affair with hundreds of women. I looked for ways to help others. Well, mostly women. For instance, if a woman looked perplexed trying to figure out how to buy a commuter card at the subway kiosk, I was quickly to her side. If my wife made comments, I would simply justify the act as kindness and tell her she was overreacting. I frequently invited women I met in public to attend church. When my wife tried to *explain* that this made her uncomfortable, I would try to make her feel unspiritual for not wanting this person to go to heaven. My wife felt like she was going crazy and I did not mind a bit if it meant I could continue my little encounters. As long as I could keep receiving a sweet "thank you" or stand close to the myriad of pretty women, I was happy with the *status quo*. I told myself I was not cheating. It wasn't an affair. Besides, I never asked for women's names or telephone numbers. Yet, inside, my wife was dying. She knew my attention and affections were diverted. She was not the only love of my life.

Eventually, I began to see all the ways that I was hiding in false intimacy and slowly strangling my marriage. By embracing the Proven Path and a lot of hard work, I put an end to all emotional type affairs. I redirected my energies back to building my relationship with the Lord and my wife.

Affairs aren't the only issue in marriage. Those turning to pornography or sexual fantasy in marriage aren't likely allowing themselves to be fully transparent with their wives. They continue to harbor secrets, perhaps fearing they would be rejected if their true nature were revealed. They're ripe for an emotional affair because that's a place with much smaller risks, where openness and communication can be carefully controlled. They don't have to be vulnerable, but can present an image that reflects how they want to be seen.

Chat Rooms and IM

Among the biggest sources of emotional affairs today are Internet chat rooms and instant messaging. It's so easy to form a connection with a woman in the controlled atmosphere of a computer. All false forms of intimacy always progress at different paces for different men. At best, emotional affairs don't satisfy the true need for intimacy and are deadly to real relationships. At worst, they progress into physical extramarital affairs.

Kent spent years escaping into lustful fantasy. He couldn't remember a time where he didn't undress pretty women with his eyes. He always turned to Internet pornography when he was bored or lonely. It became a weekend ritual culminating in masturbation. His longings for intimacy drew him to hang out in Internet chat rooms. He loved how he felt when others paid him compliments and attention.

The fire was stoked further when Kent started using Facebook to locate women from his past. He hit the jackpot when he learned that his high school sweetheart lived only 30 miles away. Although Sherry was married, he soon discovered she was not very happy. Kent gladly listened to her concerns and offered needed support. Sherry grew to enjoy the listening ear of Kent. She began thinking she had made a mistake long ago in her marriage. Kent also became obsessed with chatting with Sherry. He would constantly go to Facebook to see if she was logged in so he could send her private messages in real time. After a few weeks of logging dozens of hours of computer talk, Kent met Sherry for lunch. Before long, they went to a motel together.

At least one study predicts that nearly two out of three Christian men will have some type of an extramarital affair before they turn 40.[49] Yet, as alarming as this statistic is, no one really thinks it will happen to them.

Men don't typically set out to have an affair. Affairs are not premeditated. But on the other hand, adultery does not just happen either. It begins slowly, starting in the heart and mind. It's often years before a physical affair with someone begins. The behavior that will lead to an affair is fostered early—in the days while you are still unmarried.

Nate had been married for seven years and had two sons. The zing from his marriage was gone. All his emotional energy was spent at work or with the boys. Although he had sex with his wife every 10 days, it was neither exciting nor frequent enough to keep him feeling content. Out of curiosity, Nate dialed a 900 telephone number for the first time. Phone sex awakened in him a deeper desire and it wasn't long before he went to a prostitute. When he crossed that line, he became one of the statistics.

By the time a man engages in a physical extramarital affair, he has been indulging in sexual fantasy and other forms of false intimacy for quite some time. He turned to a pseudo relationship in place of a real relationship. But it's never truly fulfilling and always leaves you craving more. It will lead you on an ever downward spiral to places you never thought possible. The Bible tells us sin can only offer a false promise of contentment: "They commit adultery with their eyes, and their desire for sin is never satisfied."[50]

I remember the time I logged into my first Internet chat room many years ago. I was curious because of the buzz about chatting. I picked a group at random and sheepishly introduced myself as a first-time user. I weaved my way through the maze of cross talk in multiple conversations. It was almost like eavesdropping on conversations between others, yet you could join in at any moment, as if you were mingling at a party. I was cheerfully welcomed and was asked questions about myself. It wasn't long before my computer made a "ding" sound and a small window popped open. Someone was starting a private conversation! I had not even been aware of instant messaging or private chatting. My reaction was, "Wow, someone is interested in me!" I traded private messages for a few minutes before rejoining the group. After 15 minutes of chatting, one woman asked me if I ever traveled to California. A sudden tinge of guilt hit me. My conscience was throwing off warning signals that this was dangerous, so I replied, "Yes, but I am married." The woman responded, "It's only meeting for lunch." That did it. I was now terrified of what this could lead to, so I logged off.

Thinking about it afterward, that chat room meeting had been exhilarating. It was a safe place where I could present myself in any manner I chose. I could control what others knew about me, not revealing anything negative, only what was desirable. I could choose what part of me they saw. In the next session I could have portrayed myself as a man who was sensitive and slightly witty. Chatting worked all too well. I became interesting to women, some of whom wanted to meet in person. What man would not appreciate that?

Fortunately, I was also scared. I knew that I couldn't start meeting women for lunch. I saw how chatting was actually cheating on a spouse by giving of oneself emotionally to other women and that it would eventually lead to deeper sins. That was the last day I visited a chat room.

What starts out as a seemingly innocent emotional outlet often leads a person down a slippery slope. Chat rooms entice with the lure of anonymity. IM doesn't hide names, but does provide a buffer where you hide in other ways. In both, it's almost as if it were an interactive game where you can play out your fantasies with intelligent artificial life forms, as on a Star Trek *holodeck*.

In chat rooms you can keep hitting reset by going to new chat rooms where you're better appreciated, or you can change your own character at will. You can even pretend to be anything or anyone you desire. The real you never gets discovered, but you still enjoy the compliments or praises.

The problem with chat rooms and IM (and even *Facebook* or text messages) is that you're more prone to share personal, intimate matters with others—things you would never talk about in person. Married men start sharing things with women that they don't even discuss with their wives because they can do it anonymously or at a distance, with no consequences for those relationships.

Each of these computer or text tools allows you to control the content and pace of the conversations. You have time to create a witty response that would not occur in a voice conversation. You also can present yourself in a manner that is different from the way you are with your wife or in real life. You can consciously say whatever the other chatter wants to hear and present yourself as the perfect man. As you get positive reactions, you highlight their desired characteristic more and more. Emotional ties are quickly formed and you long for the next encounter.

In a way that is similar to how alcohol lowers inhibitions, computer chatting increases your daring ... and flirting. With the barriers down, you run a risk of quickly developing a kind of emotional intimacy—even though you are presenting a false self to someone else who is most likely presenting a false self too. In a curious way, you can be less guarded when you are in disguise.

These computer relationships are especially high-risk areas for men who already are looking at Internet pornography or regularly engaging in sexual fantasy. If you've already become adept at being turned on by a fantasy world, then it's easy to simply add a real person to that cyber-fantasy world through chat rooms. The lines become very blurred. Even if you know in the back of your mind that it may be wrong, you may feel irresistibly drawn to it.

It's time to flee temptation. It's time to turn away from all forms of affairs. It's time to guard your heart and decide to live a Proven and victorious life.

Singles Beware

If you're unmarried, don't think you're safe or that the section regarding post-marital affairs is not relevant. Right now you're developing styles of relating to women, including the one you will some day call your wife. Listen carefully: Your reliance on false forms of intimacy will spill over into your marriage. There's a reason why nearly two-thirds of married Christian men continue to masturbate after marriage and end up flirting with and engaging in affairs with women. Men who turn to false forms of intimacy prior to marriage tend to continue relying on false forms of intimacy after marriage. They're not learning how to properly engage in real relationships. With the habit of false intimacy, it gets harder to accept the hard work and pain that goes with real relationships.

I am not saying that a single man cannot IM or text women when unmarried, but be mindful of how a carefully controlled computer relationship can teach you to hide or hold back from true intimacy. Marriage is not a magic pill that creates a new character in you that automatically becomes open and honest with a spouse.

In the next section, you will learn the Proven Path for living a victorious life while single and married.

Passionate for God,
Repentant in spirit,
Open and honest,
Victorious in living,
Eternal in perspective, and
Networking with other *Proven Men.*

PART II

The *PROVEN* Path

Passionate for God,
Repentant in spirit,
Open and honest,
Victorious in living,
Eternal in perspective, and
Networking with other *Proven Men.*

Chapter

The Basics

Men everywhere are asking for a Proven Path for overcoming habits of sexual immorality. Some are perplexed because they have beautiful, loving wives and cannot understand the allure of pornography. Others try justifying urges because their wives withhold sex or intimacy. But each is in search of answers to a problem plaguing men for centuries: How to have freedom from sexual bondage.

Many men approach me with the similar questions because they know that I have been walking in victory for a long time. It's important to state up front that there are no magical formulas and no quick fixes. But there is a way out. *The only road to freedom from sexual obsession is an intimate and daily relationship with Jesus Christ.* If that doesn't exist, some form of sin will always tear you down. The good news is that Jesus loves you and wants to stand alongside and free you. He wants to be an active part of your life. In fact, He made you in such a way that you would daily share your life with Him.

The truth is that most men who are struggling with sexual integrity actually long to live out a Proven life. They desire to live by God's Spirit, which will keep them from gravitating to the lust of the world. Yet, most know firsthand that simply being told to pray about it or to act with more self-control doesn't usher in change. Men need training and encouragement. They need to see an example of what it takes to live pure through times of temptation.

The PROVEN acronym addresses these questions and issues. It provides a path to guide you every day in living pure in a sex-based world. That means through God's grace you can fulfill the heavenly purpose of "denying ungodliness and worldly lusts," and "live soberly, righteously, and Godly in the present age."[51] Naturally, your relationship with God is based on so much more than disengaging from certain sinful practices. It can mean joining the Lord in a true, intimate relationship. Although sexual integrity is something to strive for, it's not something you can win on your own.

For that reason, the Proven Path may not be what you expect. There's not a list of 10 things to do. There are no quick fixes or shortcuts. And it's not enough to make a one-time commitment to sexual integrity.

The key to understanding the Proven Path is found in this statement: *The by-product of a right relationship with God begins the loosening of the grip of lust and other sinful desires.* Sexual integrity is a by-product of yielding control to God. It's that simple. Victory is won through living out the fundamentals of our Christian faith and being stamped a Proven Man.

Becoming a Proven Man is a lifetime process. It depends on constantly being on guard and being renewed and changed daily—from the inside out. That's why I created an intensive 12-week companion daily study to this book, named *The 12-Week Study to a PROVEN Path to Sexual Integrity,* to infuse you with the fundamental Christian principles of living each new today in freedom as you strive for absolute purity. Plan to go through our study. Think of it as your spring training where you learn the fundamentals, but then carry those principles forward in life as you continue to grow.

The PROVEN Path

The PROVEN Path is based upon six keys for living out a Proven life:

Passionate for God,
Repentant in spirit,
Open and honest,
Victorious in living,
Eternal in perspective, and
Networked with other *Proven Men*.

Each letter of PROVEN stands for an essential element for your Christian life. When all six are combined, the entire purposes of a man are aligned. Then, the sweet voice of God whispers: "Well done, my good and faithful servant. You receive my Proven stamp." In fact, each moment you walk in step with the Lord, you won't sink into sexual sin.

▶ **JOEL: A Secret Life**

Before I became a Proven Man, almost daily I waited every night for my wife to go to sleep; then I would begin mentally downloading all the pictures I purposed to capture in my mind throughout the day. My heart would race as I scrolled through images. Who would it be tonight? I would spend nearly an hour every night conjuring up fantasies based on the women I saw that day. I might pretend the blonde invites me to her apartment or the redhead wants sex in the back seat of her car. I would come up with dozens of scenarios based on the top picks of the day, culminating in masturbation.

On other occasions, I would see one of the model's eyes while having sex with my wife. Either way, by morning guilt and shame would nip at my heels. I hated that part of this life—the guilt and shame. I tried countless times to stop masturbating. But defeating the monster of lust and its tentacle of masturbation or pornography was the one thing that eluded me in life.

If I had measured the number of invented fantasies that played in my mind while masturbating, the number would easily have reached 250,000, based on 35 lustful thoughts a day for 20 years. I had given myself over to sexual fantasy; it transcended my everyday life. I sexualized almost everything. Nearly every pretty woman I met, I undressed with my eyes or saved her image for later use.

Joel's Public Life; a World Closing in on Me

On the other hand, I was one of the nicest young men you could ever meet. I reminded myself that I didn't lie, cheat, steal, smoke, drink, or swear. And I could count on one hand the number of times I missed church. During law school, at age 27, I had accepted Jesus as Savior and had soon met a woman I fell in love with. We were married within a year. Everything was falling into place. However, the lustful thoughts and masturbation didn't go away. As I became a married Christian man, I still maintained my former fantasy life. In fact, I continued to keep opening my mind daily to sensuality. I was fixated on beautiful women in TV shows, commercials, or magazines. Even on the way to work I "noticed" (and captured their image in my mind) sensually dressed women. My constant lustful thoughts only heightened my desire more for sex, making me think I needed it every day.

Before long, my wife and I were involved in many activities at church and were viewed as a model couple. I knew I needed help, but was too proud and ashamed to ask. Yet my world seemed to be closing in on me and I needed to find a way of escape. I knew that it was just a matter of time before I would have an affair or otherwise drive my wife away—and she was too precious to lose. No matter how many times I promised myself that I would abstain, after about three weeks I would begin masturbating again. In fact, my thoughts and actions continued to grow more and more impure.

Getting Started

After I made the decision to switch masters and give up masturbation, it wasn't long before my wife and others were seeing changes in me. Several years later, my transformation was so noticeable, that I was asked to be an elder in my church. My pastor asked me to write a short article on what it was that made the difference. As I began jotting down notes I believe the Lord clearly revealed it to me by giving me the PROVEN acronym and Proven Men name. Looking back I saw clearly how I put each of these six things into my life and continue to do through the present. Yes, there is a Proven Path. It worked for me because it was not a program, but a way of getting my relationship right with the Lord. At its core, it is based on incorporating all six letters of the word PROVEN into your life.

Passionately seek God. Being passionate for the Lord is a key element of building sexual integrity. When you're caught up in sexual sin, it's hard to passionately seek and praise the Lord. That's because you are concentrating on your circumstances and seeking to fulfill your cravings for selfish pleasures. Therefore, the biggest step toward sexual integrity begins with taking the focus off you and putting it onto God. As you do, you'll see the beauty of the Lord and want to praise Him.

There's only one true, perfect and holy God. He alone deserves worship and praise. It's not difficult to praise Him. Instead, it demands a lot effort to withhold what's due to Him. Because of your innate need to worship God, your refusal to express your passion to Him by engaging in selfish pleasures can become a full-time job. It will rob you of the riches He intends for you.

Turn your desire toward the Lord. Run to the Lord who loves you unconditionally and who is the only source of true life and healing. During times of worship, the Lord imparts Himself to you. Your experience of His nature and attributes will burn away apathy, anger, self-pity, self-condemnation, and pride. You'll become holy and pure as He is holy and pure. Then your passion for the Lord will start replacing the lust for selfish desires and practices. In fact, during times of intimate worship, you'll experience God's very nature and begin receiving His healing in all areas of your life. Therefore, make it your number one goal in life to know the Lord and worship Him with all of your mind, heart and soul.

Repent from the sin of turning from God. God longs for your fellowship. He longs to welcome you. Although sin is what separates us, repentance is the Lord's gift of grace that frees us from shackles of guilt and shame so we can see the path toward restoration of our relationship with our God-friend. True repentance involves not only confessing each sin, but also turning to and submitting to God. It's time to start seeing your sin as evil—if for no other reason than because it turns you away from God. Your lust for illicit sexual activities grieves the Lord, because it treats others as objects for degradation and makes you discontent with what God provides. In short, it keeps you from seeking intimacy with Him.

Your worship of selfish pleasure is, in fact, idolatry, acted out through sexual sins, such as pornography, lust, and fantasy. Confess your selfishness and pride, which seek to elevate your needs to a throne above God. Without true repentance, you literally oppose God. Without true repentance, all of your relationships will be shallow and unfulfilling.

Until you see your sexual sin as evil—*because* it separates you from closeness to God—you won't truly want to change. Repentance is not self-manufactured. It doesn't merely emerge from feelings of guilt or shame. It's a gift from God, granted to those who humbly seek Him with all of their hearts. Therefore, weep and mourn. Cry out to God to break your stubborn, hard heart. Build repentance into your daily life and begin living for the Lord.

Open in communication with God and others. One inward reason people turn to false forms of intimacy (i.e., pornography, masturbation, or fantasy) is that it seems safer or easier than the work required in real, open and honest relationships. But your heart and soul inwardly long for true intimacy. Fortunately, God will enable you to fully trust. He will also teach you how to be open and to permit feelings to surface so you can engage in fulfilling and real relationships, instead of escaping into the false forms of intimacy that have ensnared you.

If you want to live out sexual integrity, end the pretense. No longer say that you hate sexual sin, while secretly enjoying it. Turn away from *false intimacy* and be willing to accept the pain that goes along with real relationships. Begin with the single greatest relationship you can and must have: unity with God. Start talking openly to the Lord. Treat Him as a living being who longs to relate to you. Stop praying at God, instead of communicating with Him. Tell the Lord of your hurts. Tell Him what troubles you. Ask questions and listen for answers. Be real … be vulnerable … be purposeful in getting to know God on a personal basis.

Be willing to ask God to expose any underlying issues in your life or sources of pain that keep you fleeing from intimacy and from turning to Him. Talk about your desire for *absolute purity* and your need for the Lord to carry out your commitments.

Brothers, it's time for you to be open and honest with yourself and with God. As you do, the need to escape into a fantasy world will shrink. Part of the process is allowing yourself to have and experience feelings, rather than stuffing them away. Yet, don't let feelings become your master. You need not give in to anger, greed, or lust.

It's equally important for you to begin modeling openness with your relationships with others. You were created to experience intimacy with real people. Push through the painful moments and become open and honest internally and externally.

In short, it's time to stop pretending. As you open up to the Lord and others, real relationships will become fulfilling and replace the façade of false intimacy, which cannot deliver on the promise of love without pain.

Victorious living in God's strength. You cannot overcome temptation or defeat lust in your own strength. Yet, by daily guarding your heart and turning to Christ, you'll lead a victorious life. Each moment you yield to the Lord and rely upon His power, your actions become pure and holy as He is pure and holy. He won't lead you into, but through temptation while in charge of your life!

God grants you a way of escape. Rely on it. As you live by His Spirit, you will live in victory.[52] It's only when you take back control that you fall into sin. When tempted, take captive the sinful thought and cut it to shreds. Don't take any pleasure from any lustful thoughts. Each and every time you stumble, return to

God right away in confession and seek His forgiveness. You'll be immediately restored.

It's time to reject performance-based thinking and self-condemnation. As you accept God's mercy and unconditional love, you'll want to remain in His camp and under His wing. Stop trying by your own efforts alone. Become the needy, dependent servant you actually are! Then, only then, will you taste His lasting victory.

Eternal in your perspective. Dwelling on the temporary (your present circumstances) leads to acting according to immediate thoughts and desires. Taking on an eternal perspective, however, brings hope and perseverance during temptations and trials. By looking to God's promises and allowing Him to be your guide, you'll live out integrity. You'll no longer be worn out from chasing temporary pleasures or defeated from the constant battle of trying to control life.

The thinking of man is futile and leads to sin. As you focus upon your circumstances, you become consumed with yourself. What rights do you so desperately protect that you'd rather live apart from God and under His care? Fifty years from now, what will matter? Put into practice "truth therapy,"[53] the act of believing God's Word over the lies and false promises of the world. To do so, you'll need to daily read and dwell upon the many precious promises in Scripture.

Ask God for wisdom and to give you His perspective. Begin seeing trials as opportunities to grow. Accept that God will not give you more than you can bear and that He always provides a way of escape; so, look for it and rely upon it. Keep your center of gravity, based upon your home and your citizenship in heaven. It'll provide you with the proper perspective when temptations seem so tempting that you contemplate throwing away your integrity.

Networked with other *Proven Men*. You were created for relationships. As you experience greater intimacy with God, you'll naturally begin connecting with others of like heart and faith. True networking (seeking out and engaging with others on a vulnerable level) provides a way of living out your real purposes. Other Proven Men become great sources of encouragement. Become part of the team!

Remember, the Lord sent out His disciples two-by-two. So, don't try to go it alone. Because you were created for relationships you'll not have rest in your soul simply by reading a purity book by yourself. You need to allow others to see past the exterior of your life. As iron sharpens iron, so do two Godly men.[54] Therefore, determine to engage with other men in open and vulnerable relationships. For instance, attend church because you want to meet the Lord and engage in corporate worship. Join a men's Bible group in order to encourage and be encouraged in living out a Christian life.

Without a *networking partner*—someone who will encourage and even hold you accountable—your pride can return unchecked and lead to selfish, sexual sins. Don't cut short the opportunity of receiving God's PROVEN stamp by missing out on this networking.

If you dismiss this last element, you're only fooling yourself that you're living out the first five elements. It's the same pride that won't allow you to confess your imperfections to another man that keeps you from being *passionate* for anything except yourself, that keeps you from truly receiving God's gift of *repentance*, that keeps you from being *open* with others, that keeps you from trusting God to provide *victory*, and keeps you from seeing life from an *eternal perspective* instead of the moment in life in which you find yourself.

It's the failure to embrace God's version of *networking* with other Proven Men that will keep you defeated and trapped in bondage to sin.

▶ TIM: Hiding in the Closet

Long before he had the vision to see that God could provide the victory in his life, Tim struggled in constant bondage to the idea that he had to prove himself with his efforts alone. His whole world revolved around his performance: "Am I good enough? Can I measure up to the standard?" If Tim failed to be perfect in anything, he was the first to beat himself up. He lived in constant stress, wondering when he would fail next. In his mind he treated himself as his father would have, assuming that his efforts were still not up to par because he probably could have done it better or faster.

His only escape was pornography. All Tim needed to do was flip through the pages and select one of many willing lovers. This fantasy world allowed Tim to escape reality. It would be the safe place where he would never have to hear that he was no good or disappoint anyone. The pleasure of masturbation confirmed that this was the world to remain hidden in. It was far safer living in a fantasy world than risk further rejection. Tim turned to masturbation in place of open relationships. He would sneak magazines to his bedroom closet so he would never be alone again.

As with all sin, its pleasures were temporary. Tim's self-condemnation for escaping into his closet robbed him of real pleasure in life. Any measure of appreciation from a real person was met with skepticism. Internally, Tim knew better. He was not worthy. Tim's biggest fear was that he would be eventually found out. Like so many others addicted to sex, Tim was plagued with the assumption that "if others really knew me, they would not like me." Tim reasoned that if his father had hated what he saw in Tim, everyone else must hate his imperfections, too. He couldn't trust his feelings or share his thoughts with anyone. It would be best not to allow anyone inside. Therefore, Tim made a vow to never tell another human soul that he masturbated.

Sinking Ship

Tim's assumption that he was no good made him vow never to date when he was in the Christian boarding school where his father sent him. Even though Tim heard the words of the Gospel of love and peace at school, he assumed it was for others, not him. It never broke the barriers of his closed heart.

As an adult, the constant strain of failing to meet his dad's expectations was met with a bottle of booze at night and frequent trips to the bathroom during the day to lose himself in pornography and masturbation. Tim would work twelve hours, then go straight to the bar. Soon Tim began going to strip clubs. For $120 per hour, a real woman would sit next to Tim and talk. They never had sex or even talked of sex, but it was the closest thing to intimacy Tim ever had.

The Underlying Basis for the *PROVEN* Path

Each of these six letters is vital to building sexual integrity. In the past, just like me, you tried using your own strength. This is self-reformation and it doesn't work. Now, it's time to turn to and rely upon God. The companion 12-week study is sometimes referred to as *Heartwork* because it really goes after a man's heart through daily reflection. It's designed to position you to meet with the Lord each day and be internally changed by Him. In fact, a person's sinful conduct changes only when his heart toward God changes. You must spend time building these elements into your life.

It's time to stop striving in your own power and give up control to the Lord. That means you must really want to turn from sin and live out a Proven life of holiness in dependence upon the Lord. This is the beginning of a passionate and fulfilling relationship with the One true God who loves you and the start of lasting freedom from bondage to sexual sin.

Distinctiveness and Ultimate Purpose

What makes the Proven Path distinctive is that it's built upon this principle: *Purity of actions will follow—not lead—the course of lasting healing.* The focus isn't upon behavior modification, but upon the shifting of your internal desires. Consider this passage:

> *Since you died with Christ to the basic principles of this world, why, as though you still belonged to it, do you submit to its rules: "Don't handle! Don't taste! Don't touch!"? These are all destined to perish with use, because they are based on human commands and teachings. Such regulations indeed have an appearance of wisdom, with their self-imposed worship, their false humility and their harsh treatment of the body, but they lack any value in restraining sensual indulgence.[55]*

As you can see, the Bible warns that following rules or trusting in programs simply does nothing to address the internal sensual desire, which leads to sinful conduct. Instead, the healing path begins with an internal heart shift that desires and purposes to live out an overall Proven life.

▶ **STAN: Clean Outside of the Cup**

Stan had never really considered the possibility of living a Proven life. Growing up, Stan had had to memorize Scripture better than others, behave better than others, and sacrifice better than others. As a "PK" (pastor's kid), Stan lived in a glass house. But it wasn't all that bad. His parents remained married and loved him. Stan learned early that he received the most praise when he followed the rules or set an example. He excelled at putting on a good face. Stan was pleased to sing songs at church because

73

everyone clapped and the older ladies would always give him praises. Everyone told his parents what a treasure they had in Stan.

Life was simple. It had one rule: Stay out of trouble. As long as no one complained to his dad, everything was good at home. Of course, Stan's dad was busy meeting everyone else's needs, which left little time for Stan. Therefore, Stan grew to entertain himself. Knowing that it's best not to let others see his inside, it didn't take too long for Stan to figure out the allure of Internet pornography and a fantasy life.

Every naked or scantily dressed woman in the pictures was wearing the same smile. You know the one—the ministry smile: "No matter what you feel inside, always smile and say everything is great." As Stan stared at the computer images of women smiling at him, Stan felt good. They made no demands of him. They were there to fulfill his every need and meet all of his desires. They never judged him nor demanded anything. It was perfect. Adding masturbation to the mix, he was hooked. Nothing felt so good. It made up for all the things he had to do to please everyone else. Even when doing the jobs at church his dad made him do because no one else would do them, Stan knew his private reward was waiting for him.

Marry Missy or Miss Out?

During college, when Stan began dating Missy, a new world opened to him. He was infatuated with her and she with him. They couldn't stand to be apart. Everything about her was fresh and exciting. Her touch was electric. Each stare increased his hormone level, so that when he was with Missy, all he could think about was unbuttoning her blouse. Deep down, Stan wanted purity, but the tug of the ecstasy of the moment was so hard to give up. Then one day he crossed the line. After that, neither he nor Missy could claim to be virgins even under the most liberal definition. It didn't take too long before Missy was feeling guilty. She was certain she would be a virgin when she married. Now that was lost—lost at the hands of Stan. Their relationship was crumbling. Stan feared she might break up with him.

Where could Stan turn? He couldn't tell his father that he is addicted to pornography or that he is having sex before marriage. His dad might call him before the elders for the laying on of hands. He was sure he would be judged by them if the sin didn't just go away once they prayed for him. In addition, there was never any sermon about sex or any other evidence that his dad or the church would realize that it takes time to change and heal. Stan had to figure out a solution himself. Fortunately, his skill with the computer landed him at the Proven Men website. All he had to do was join, but that would mean admitting his practices. It was a hard decision to make.

Sexual integrity does not and cannot rely upon human effort as its primary source of power or strength. You know this verse: "Unless the Lord builds the house, they labor in vain who build it."[56] That means victory occurs when a man turns over control—complete control—of his heart and life to the Lord. Only then does he enter into the exchanged life spoken of in Galatians 2:20, which states:

> *I have been crucified with Christ; It's no longer I who live, but Christ lives in me; and the life which I now live in the flesh I live by faith in the Son of God, who loved me and gave Himself for me.*

This verse has particular application regarding living victoriously over sexual sins, even in the heat of the battle with temptation.

For instance, living a Proven life is all about asking and allowing Christ to live in and through you. Only a heart-change (changing your desires from the inside out) results in true purity of thought and deed.

My dear brother, won't you embrace living out a Proven life, and won't you join with other Proven Men in building sexual integrity? It's time to start walking the Proven Path.

Chapter

Build a Strong Foundation

You've been given a good look at the big picture and your need to be stamped PROVEN. Now, let's focus on some of the fundamentals of your faith in order to establish a firm foundation.

Are you ready to begin building sexual integrity? Then take the time to wrestle with and own the concepts in this chapter, as they're the essential building blocks upon which the entire process is based. Even if some are familiar, don't skip over them. Future chapters build upon them. This is the same set of foundations I use with every man I minister to.

Laying a Foundation

The first foundational principle is best understood by answering a question. "Why did God created people in the first place?" Don't gloss over it. Answer in your mind right now: "Why did God create you?"

Don't worry if you aren't sure or if your answer is a bit different from what will be described below. But do pay close attention to the answer. This is the start of your understanding of why you're tempted to lust. And this understanding is the first step in building sexual integrity. In short, you must first understand the purpose of your genuine relationship with God before you can see the root problem for the division of that relationship that attacks your sexual integrity.

Twin Purposes

The answer that is you were created for two purposes. The first is to worship God.[57] Now, while that does mean bringing glory to God, it must be genuine. The Lord could have made you a robot reciting praise platitudes all day long, but that would not be true worship. God wants you to love Him freely and for you to realize that He is perfect and worthy of praise.

Think of it this way. It wasn't wrong to create you to worship God because He also created you to experience joy in the presence of perfection. You may experience the most sublime joy in any number of ways. When your favorite team wins a game, you may literally shout for joy. When you truly make love with your wife, you may experience a transcendent joy that fills you with happiness. Magnificent mountains, luminous sunsets, beautiful works of art and all the great creations of God and man are meant to give you joy. The birth of a child, the embrace of a loved one, the laughter of dear friends are joyful moments, too.

Yet God is more amazing and perfect than anything in this world. That is why the purest form of joy you can experience is through worshiping the Lord.

The second reason you were created is to have an intimate relationship with God. You have been given an official invitation not only to visit, but forever to dwell in the house of the Lord, the Creator of the Universe. This is a pretty awesome purpose for your life.

There are actually two aspects of this relationship. First, you're called to be a son of God,[58] which occurs when you trust Jesus as Savior. Remarkably, God wants to adopt you as a son and make you His heir.[59] The divine invitation doesn't end there. God also calls you to be His friend.[60] It is one thing for God to admire you as His own creation but quite another for Him to want to be your best friend.

Think about the definition of a friend for a moment:

> *A person whom one knows well and is fond of; intimate associate; close acquaintance [or] a person on the same side in a struggle; one who is not an enemy or foe.*[61]

As incredible as it sounds, God invites you into divine intimacy with Him as an "intimate associate." It also means God not only knows you well, but is on the same side as you during your struggles. Now that's a friend!

Let's recap. You were created to have two special kinds of relationships with God. Go ahead and hold up your first two fingers on your left hand to denote these two purposes for why God created you. Look at your left index finger and say, "I was created to worship God." Now say to the next finger on that hand, "I was created to have a friendship relationship with God." Hold those thoughts for a moment.

▶ **JOEL: Escape from Temptation**

When did it all start? When I was twelve, I found a *Playboy* magazine hidden under a bed. As I looked at the pictures of the naked women, I began fantasizing about sex. In fact, I soon became fixated on sex. I began seeing women as objects of desire. I developed a lifestyle of masturbating almost daily while thinking about sexual images or fantasies. Although I felt guilty afterward, each night as I closed my eyes sexual thoughts flooded my mind and I would begin the ritual all over again.

In high school I actually went to an X-rated movie and even to a topless bar. At 18, I bought a few *Playboy* magazines, as well as some hard-core pornography. But more than those things, my issue was that sex was always on my mind. I didn't need the stimulus of pornography because I could easily find sexual images or ideas almost everywhere. It was my mind that was polluted. I purposefully stored images in my mind of faces or bodies of women I met during the day to use for masturbation at night.

During college I began having sex. This only fueled the fire more. I continued to fantasize and masturbate. Each relationship ultimately ended without satisfaction. Although deep down I knew lustful thoughts and masturbation were wrong, I held on to the belief that, as soon as I got married, it would stop. It didn't. Even seven years into my marriage, I was regularly lusting and masturbating.

After I married, I knew I needed to stop dreaming of sex with other women. Naturally, I first relied upon my own efforts. I took cold showers and even sought sex with my wife daily. But the intense desire for "just a little bit more" was never quenched. Repeatedly, I vowed to put an end to masturbation. Yet, it merely ushered in fresh rounds of failure, guilt and shame, as vow after vow was broken. Nothing had worked because none of my actions addressed the root issues giving rise to the sensual desire, and none of my efforts relied on the strength of the Lord.

Although I believed my intentions to be good, at the core, my motive for asking God to remove the temptation was not pure. I didn't want to replace false intimacy with real and open relationships. I still wanted love without the pain associated with real relationships. I believed sex to be my own unmet need and equated sex with love. This lie kept me in bondage to sexual sin for many years. I was growing tired of my secret life of a double agent and constant failure. It wasn't until I was close to having a physical affair that I conceded I would never be able to climb my way to freedom on my own. I was finally willing to ask for help.

Admitting the Problem

In the end, I became so afraid of acting out on one of my thousands of sexual fantasies and actually committing adultery that I went to the pastor of my church and admitted that I had a sex problem that I couldn't overcome. The pastor didn't reject me, but cried with me and hugged me. He reassured me and told me that he loved me. I couldn't believe the pastor didn't judge me or throw me out of church. It marked a new direction for me. I felt a great weight had been lifted. I even dared to harbor the thought, "If the pastor didn't reject me, maybe my wife or God won't either." I went home and confessed to my wife all of my sins—my sexual fantasies, selfishness and my pride—and went through 12 weeks of Biblical counseling for sexual integrity. After that, I was finally willing to surrender this one last area of my life to God.

Willing to do whatever it took, I began meeting weekly with a man who had overcome sexual addiction himself. He reassured me that it was possible to live in freedom. I knew there was much work ahead, but I also knew there was hope. I was 100 percent committed to being changed by God and willing to do whatever it took to live a pure life in dependency upon Him.

The more I surrendered to God and began allowing Christ to live through me, the more the Lord carried me to purity and a place of rest. The Proven Path opened an entire new and rich manner of knowing God and provided tools for seeking after the Lord with all of my heart. But don't misunderstand. It was a lot of work and I was in for the fight of my life.

Two Greatest Commands

The Bible is God's roadmap to show you the way to live out your twin purposes in life. The Lord doesn't want you to go through life ignorant or constantly fighting against your purposes.

Consider this. On one particular occasion, the Pharisees sent their best lawyer to try to trap Jesus. This is what he asked: "Teacher, which is the great commandment in the law?"[62] The very question showed a heart already off track. It was based upon the faulty premise that if a man kept the most important laws, which the Pharisees thought they were doing, he would be considered righteous; whereas a swindler, like a tax collector who violated the most important laws, would not.[63]

The answer Jesus gave was astonishing. In fact, in doing so, Christ confirmed man's twin purposes for being created and the real purpose for the commands in Scripture.

> *'You shall love the Lord your God with all your heart, with all your soul, and with all your mind.' This is the first and great commandment. And the second is like it: 'You shall love your neighbor as yourself.' On these two commandments hang all the Law and the Prophets.*[64]

Jesus was not constrained by the question asking for the single most important law, and He gave not one, but two commandments in response. He did this so you would know your twin purposes in life. Taking it even further, Christ then tied these two principles together with everything the prophets of God had been teaching from the beginning.

Although the question was a designed trap, Jesus didn't pass up the opportunity to teach His followers that the true purpose for all of Scripture was to show us how to live out our twin purposes in life. Christ confirmed that the chief end of man is to worship God and love his neighbors!

If you will now hold out two fingers on your right hand, these fingers will represent the two greatest commands. To your right index finger say, "I must love God with all of my heart, soul and mind." To the middle finger say, "I must love others." (This certainly provides a new meaning to your middle finger, often used to convey hatred toward others!)

Now, I'd like to use your hands to demonstrate how the concept of your two purposes for being created and the two greatest commands in all of Scripture dovetail together. Hold out the same two fingers on both hands. Bring them close together. Do you see the resemblances between your two purposes for being created and the two commands upon which the entire Bible hangs?

The first finger on the left tells you: "I was created to worship God," while the first finger on the right reminds you that the greatest command in the Bible is, "I must love God with all of my heart, soul and mind." They are fulfilled in the same way!

The next finger on the left tells you, "I was created to have a friendship relationship with God," and the same finger on your right hand says that, in order to do so, "I must love others." It's by loving others that you fully live out your friendship with God. You cannot be God's friend without also loving those He created in His image. According to the Bible, anyone who says he loves God but hates his brother is a liar.[65] If you're allowing Christ to live through you, you'll love others because Christ loves them.

Think of it this way, what kind of friend would you be if you told someone, "I love you but I hate your son"? Take it a step further. How often would someone keep inviting you over if, after each meal, you kicked his infant? Relationships bind together your "friendship" purpose with the second command to be a friend to God's children!

Now bring your hands together. Intertwine and overlap the two left and two right fingers. Lock these fingers together into a snug fit. Notice how tight the connection is between them. The same is true with these concepts.

Isn't it incredible how God unifies your twin purposes for living and the two-fold plan of the Bible? God gave you the entire Bible—not so you could be legalistic or feel defeated, but so you would have guidance for living out your twin purposes for being created: to love God and others. With it you certainly have enough information to experience real life as He designed it for you. Real fruit and freedom reign when you stop fighting against your true purposes in life.

▶ TIM: Condemnation

At his lowest emotional point, Tim's weight rose to 300 pounds. He had no expectations of ever dating a girl or pleasing his dad. Tim couldn't risk another rejection. He would retreat into fantasy, porn and masturbate himself to sleep every night.

Tim knew the basic Bible verses from Sunday school. But his idea of being crucified with Christ meant to debase himself with condemning thoughts. Throughout his life, his dad kept telling him he would never amount to anything. Tim knew he could never measure up, so he frequently stopped trying. Adding more burden to his soul was Tim's view that taking up the cross of Christ meant carrying the load himself. He was always burdened and defeat was his constant companion.

Tim eventually did get married to the first girl he dated—a woman from work who asked him out, but he hid from her his feelings, hopes and dreams. Tim was constantly pretending to be someone else and never let his guard down. The drinking and masturbation continued in full force. Tim felt certain that he didn't deserve a wife so beautiful and caring. He had no idea what she saw in him. Since Tim couldn't afford to risk losing her, it was simple: "I must never let her see the real me."

They attended church each week and she became quite active in women's ministries. Tim pretended to be spiritual and learned the Christian talk. However, whenever she left for a meeting, Tim would shout, "I am free!" That meant drinking and watching pornography. What happened next was every man's worst nightmare. Tim's wife came home early one night to find a XXX-rated DVD on the coffee table. His wife looked at him with tears flowing from her eyes as she held the DVD and asked him "Why?" He knew why, but he couldn't tell her. He couldn't let her inside. He couldn't reveal his fears.

Tim was at a crossroads. His wife was going to leave if he didn't attend Proven Men. The choice was hard, but Tim thought he could fake another phase of his life. He was a master at it. Tim would attend in person, but continue to conceal his heart. He could never admit his failure. He would be destroyed if anyone learned that he was so messed up that he had to masturbate up to 10 times a day just to cope with reality.

Understanding Your Role

Sexual sins violate both of your purposes for living. It's no wonder you feel shame and lack lasting peace when you sacrifice sexual integrity. You're fighting against your very nature.

Are you ready to embrace your true role in life? The more you see the Lord for who He is—your master builder and best friend—the more you'll desire your wonderful opportunity for a relationship with Him. By living out all six elements of a Proven life, you'll fulfill your twin purposes in life and be free from bondage to sin because your new desire will be climbing God's holy mountain to be with Him.

You Never Call, You Never Write...

Suppose you have a son who is going to win the Nobel Peace Prize. Although he lives in the same town, he's so busy at work that he never visits, he never writes, he never calls. All you know about him these days is what you read in the newspaper. I know you would be proud of him, but wouldn't you rather your son talk with you, give you a hug, and tell you that he loves you?

The same is true for God. He's not satisfied sitting in heaven reading a newspaper about your life. He doesn't say, "Oh good, I see that Tim doesn't masturbate anymore," or "Ah, yes, it says that Joel didn't look with lust at women on his commute" or "Wonderful, Stan didn't have sex with his girlfriend today."

God wants to have an intimate relationship with you. He wants you to talk to Him about everything. He wants you to tell Him of your struggles with lust, to tell Him of your worries, to ask Him for help, to talk about your desires and needs, and to tell Him you love Him.

It's not enough that you set as a goal to stop looking at porn or quit another sexual sin. God created you for a relationship with Him, not just to avoid sin or go off on your own doing good works or even winning the Nobel Peace Prize. You were designed to experience an intimate daily relationship with God. Until you do, you'll always have something missing in your life that you'll try filling with things, such as sex, work, sports, hobbies, or other forms of entertainment.

Be Holy, As I Am Holy

In living out a Proven life, God discloses that you must do this one thing: "Be holy, for I am holy."[66] Why do you think God included this requirement in His instructional book? Why would He want you to be holy as He is holy? Fortunately, God is not challenging you to a holiness competition or laying in wait to smack you down every time you fail. Nor is He looking down from heaven, at a distance, keeping a holiness tally.

His motive is not to get your good deeds to outweigh the bad. God wants to enter into a relationship with you. He is a loving Father—worthy of being a friend—not a harsh taskmaster keeping score. The true meaning of this verse, "Be holy for I am holy," is actually a beautiful invitation to join with God as one.

Your New Best Friend

Have you ever had a best friend, who was so close that you sometimes knew what he was thinking? Even by looking into his eyes, you could tell what he was going to say next. To have that kind of a friendship, you usually need to spend a lot of time together.

This is precisely the kind of relationship God wants with you. He invites you to spend time with Him, enjoying Him as your own best friend. He knows that the more time you spend with Him, the more you will fall in love with Him, because He is perfect. He will offer you His unconditional love, not coercion, to draw you to His side.

Image that your best friend lived some distance from you. For some reason he could never leave that city, but he wanted to spend time with you. Wouldn't you willingly go to that city so you could sit next to him and engage him face-to-face? God is like that friend in that He can never stop being holy. No matter how much He wants to spend time with you, He cannot come to you, if you are in places of unholiness. Therefore, in order for you to be with God you must put aside all that's unholy and go to Him. That's why God is calling you to move from impurity to purity—to *be holy, as He is holy*—so that you can spend time together.

Accept God's invitation to unite as one. Let it spur you toward a desire to know the true nature of your heavenly Father, who loves you dearly and softly invites you into His inner court. It's out of pure love that the Heavenly Father wants you to be just like Him, *holy*. How precious and how wonderful are His ways when you can see what they are that He intends!

▶ STAN: Lack of Intimacy with God

It took Stan a long time to see the love his Heavenly Father wanted to give him. Stan was filled with head knowledge, but never truly knew the power of the Scriptures or the meaning of a deep intimate relationship with God. Despite his upbringing in the church, he needed a spiritual heart transplant. Stan needed to actually trust in God and surrender his will for his future to the Lord. Being unable to stop having sexual contact with his beloved girlfriend was what it took for Stan to understand that God couldn't be bargained with and that true Christianity required total surrender.

Stan began reading testimonies and stories on the website of Proven Men about men—men just like himself. Contacting them seemed like a risk he could afford. After all, this way his dad and no one from church would even know about it—about his secrets. But it wasn't that easy. Stan still had to battle his pride. At first, Stan wondered why he should attend a dozen group meetings. He was not thrilled about adding yet another Bible study to his menu. Stan certainly knew more about the Bible than the man leading. Ultimately, Stan decided to sign up because he knew he needed to do something, anything. After all, he wanted to keep Missy.

New Relationships with God

Stan figured that a confidential small group of men was a risk he could afford. Stan committed that he would work through the *Study,* and weekly join in accountability with others sharing the same struggle. After all, it was only for 12 weeks. He reminded himself that he could bail if it was too boring.

Something remarkable began to happen. Stan was able to share anything in that small group without a single person judging him. He didn't have to pretend to be perfect. This was new territory for Stan, so he stuck around.

After several weeks of going through the *Study,* Stan's heart began to melt. Tears even came to his eyes. He couldn't believe it. Stan had memorized Scripture for years, but had never known its true power or the real meaning of an intimate relationship with God. But now Stan was experiencing a new relationship with God.

One night at group he shook his head and told the leader, "I cannot believe it. The message of the Gospel is so simple. I finally get it." Stan was stunned at the simplicity of the Proven Path, how it really did capture the Christian walk. He had thought that his years of study would bring him closer to God, but only now was Stan yielding his life and beginning to live out the simple Gospel.

Stan wanted to be stamped PROVEN—not to earn a reward, but to know the Lord intimately. He now wanted to obey instead of play religion. Stan was committed to being open and honest, instead of posing. He wanted real relationships. He wanted to know God as a real person. Stan also began to recognize that sexual integrity was worth the price, that being faithful to the Lord was worth more than anything else. He was also beginning to understand that premarital sex hindered and damaged relationships, even after marriage. He wanted to know—truly know—Missy. And once he could accept that God was not holding out on him, it fortified him to wait for sex until he was married. He started to see that true intimacy must come first.

The Root Cause for Sexual Sin

It's time to unveil another hidden aspect of sexual sin that keeps men from living out a Proven life. Look at your right hand. This time, imagine each finger as a sin. Your index finger is pornography, the next finger is masturbation, the next is greed, the next is judgmental attitudes, and the last is jealousy.

Some people can, out of sheer determination, bend over one of the fingers to reduce the size of the sin. Maybe some can even bend over two fingers. But there are still other fingers of sin in your life.

Chances are pretty good that if you are holding in or suppressing sensual desires—white knuckling it, so to speak—something like anger or greed will pop up in its place. For most, pornography or masturbation will simply return when their strength fails.

Do you think that God is pleased because one or two fewer sins are present? Don't you agree that He would rather be invited into your life to help you with these struggles, and show you His way out?

Suppose that in your right palm lies the root of your lust, pornography, masturbation, greed, jealousy, and anger. If you knew the source of that root, you could do something about it. Well, all these sins stem from selfishness and pride.[67]

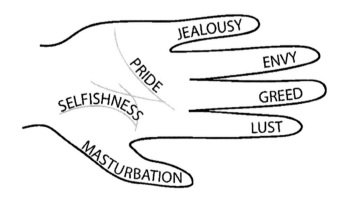

It's your selfishness that keeps you from living a Proven life. You become so consumed with your rights and circumstances that you lose sight of the real prize. Then your pride keeps you from being willing to do whatever it takes to be pure, because that means you give up control to God and begin trusting Him. As long as selfishness and pride dominate you, you'll always be a slave to some form of sexual sin and other "self" motivated sin, like greed and anger.

What you need is an antidote for pride and selfishness. The next chapter will give you the fundamentals for healing and lasting change.

BE ON GUARD.

Passionate for God,
Repentant in spirit,
Open and honest,
Victorious in living,
Eternal in perspective, and
Networking with other *Proven Men.*

Chapter

Make a Heart Shift

You've now been introduced to many concepts regarding the building blocks for sexual integrity. But information won't transform you. It must sink deep into your heart. You must own it. You must make a heart shift—a decision to change and be changed by the Lord.

Are You Selfish and Proud?

A critical self-examination is in order. If pride and its companion, selfishness, are the roots that fuel fantasy and illicit lust, isn't it time you gauged how much they take control of you?

Step back and examine your heart. Look closely at your life for evidence of pride. Take notice of the ways you think and behave selfishly. As you do, it will become more and more obvious just how much pride and selfishness exist in your life. As part of this process, it's important to ask God to open your eyes to it. Then allow yourself to see the truth, no matter how surprising and unpleasant it may seem.

Most men can easily see selfish behavior in the life of others, but it's hard to see it in their own lives. If that's true for you, consider these examples of selfishness. Do they sound familiar?

- *wanting to be the first in line*
- *choosing the best piece of food*
- *talking more than you listen*
- *insisting others abide by your own preferences*
- *allowing others to give to you, without giving to them in return*

Pride is also visible when you dominate conversations, focus your concerns on yourself, protect your own rights and not those of others, refuse to overlook wrongs, withhold forgiveness, engage in boastfulness, put others down, and complain. How quickly are you to judge or find fault in others?

Ouch! Do you see some of these things in your life?

Let's continue deeper. Your fantasy life itself can reveal the deep roots of selfishness and pride in your life. Most fantasies are built on selfish, prideful longings to be served and have your every desire satisfied. Even when you daydream, aren't you the hero or the star?

Although we all experience pride, not everyone exhibits pride in the same ways. For instance, some men are shy or even fearful. They may even consider themselves dumb compared to others. Like Tim, they may feel like misfits. Yet even those who engage in self-condemnation often act out of pride. Their insecurity, fear, self-doubt or self-loathing lead them to beat themselves down and refuse to accept love *because* they don't measure up to a prideful idea of perfection. They place their pride in the image of perfection they believe they should achieve and then despise themselves for not being perfect—so much so that they punish themselves with condemning thoughts and words. It may seem strange that those who are so determined to condemn themselves are actually caught up in the same root of selfishness and pride, but ask yourself this: Would someone who was truly humble be so self-obsessed? Would they hold themselves to such a high standard that they couldn't possibly achieve it? Those who claim to be "the worst in the world" make themselves just as "special" as those who claim to be the best. It's the inverse expression of the same preoccupation with self.

▶ Tim: Pride, Posing as Low Self-Esteem

Tim made sure he came to each Proven Men meeting. In fact, Tim's wife had it marked on the calendar so he couldn't "forget." At first, the 12-week study was more than Tim could handle. Of course that was partly because each night Tim was still watching TV at 2:00 a.m. to escape reality, leaving him no time to complete the exercises in the study.

But there was something about attending the weekly group meetings that allured him. It was the first place he could tell someone he was a mess and not get beaten up. No matter how much he shared, he was not judged. His heart was beginning to soften. He frequently cried during the group as new feelings kept surfacing. Tim now actually longed to be made well.

Tim generally understood how pride was a main root that fueled sexual sins. But was he also filled with pride? Initially he couldn't believe it. How could a person with such a low self-esteem be proud? As he reflected more, he could see how his self-condemnation was actually another manifestation of pride. Because Tim couldn't stand not being perfect, he often didn't even try.

For instance, because he didn't think his advertisements were perfect, he didn't send any out to attract new customers. Each time he didn't measure up to perfection, he beat himself up. Even in the area of sex, his pride had been the root problem. He started to see that because he didn't get what he "deserved," he indulged himself in masturbation. He also saw how his escape into fantasy was based in pride, posing as low self-esteem, like a wolf in sheep's clothing.

It was the fear of not being seen as perfect that caused Tim to hide in fantasy and false intimacy. Dealing with his pride would be hard and it would take time to undo his self-condemnation, but Proven Men gave him the right start and the Lord will finish the work in him.

The lists of examples of pride could go on. But you know yourself. You may be like Joel, puffed up and full of himself, or like Tim who continues to punish himself with his dad's lies, or you may be somewhere in between. Every one of us struggles with pride.

If you refuse to admit that you are filled with pride and selfishness, you're not ready for sexual integrity. That's right. You'll see no reason to stop striving by your own strength, pulling harder at your bootstraps to pick yourself up. Until you embrace that you are puffed up, you might simply keep drifting from program to program, until finding something to tickle your ears.[68] You're only willing to do things your way, even as you strive for purity. But you won't build true sexual integrity because the Lord's healing always escapes the proud. In fact, the Bible says that when you are guided by pride, you are acting as an enemy of God.[69] Be warned—the Bible clearly states that God opposes the proud, but gives grace to the humble.[70]

A common denominator for those willing to turn from sexual sins and begin building sexual integrity is a heart-based recognition about just how much selfishness and pride is present in their lives. Before this veil is lifted they march on blindly as enemies of God, joining the common ranks of the world.

Perhaps you're still unsure if you're proud. Do you need convincing that you're selfish? Examine the next list of ways these qualities show themselves. Ask God to open your eyes to your foolish pride, so you may finally fall on your knees in sorrow and take on a servant's heart so the wellspring of life will flood your being with a new spirit of humility and bring forth in you a Proven life totally aligned with the will of God. Consider these additional examples of pride:

- *seeking the best seat at an event*
- *comparing yourself to others*
- *coveting a larger TV or new car*
- *desiring praise, but rarely complimenting others*
- *wanting to be waited upon*
- *expecting to be noticed*
- *selecting high-profile positions at church, work, or in the community*
- *considering yourself better than others*
- *finding fault in others*
- *living without concern for the needy, suffering, or poor*
- *dreaming of an easy life*
- *thinking you'll escape consequences others face for similar conduct*
- *being quick to justify your actions*
- *refusing to give God the first fruits of your time, affection and resources*

Dear brothers, fall prostrate in repentance. Confess your stubborn pride and selfish practices and turn to the Lord. See your pride through the eyes of the Lord and realize the need to put an end to selfishness.

The Antidote

What's the antidote to pride? How do you stop being selfish? You must know by now that you can't prevail in the strength of your own hands. It boils down to this: You must give up control to Christ. You need to yield your entire life to the Lord—every square inch.

Remember how you designated the palm of your own hand as the root of pride and selfishness. Compare it now to Christ's hands on the cross. Nails pierced through his hands. Yet it was not the nails, but Christ's perfect humility that held Him to the cross. Even after Christ arose, He chose to keep the scars of the nails to bear witness to a doubting Thomas.[71] Let these same scars remind you to die to yourself and relinquish your selfishness and pride.

▶ JOEL: Letting Go of Pride

Early on in the process, my wife was not so sure that I would change. After all, I had been unfaithful to her in my heart from Day One of our marriage. I still remember clearly something she told me that helped change the course of my life: "You are just sorry about the consequences, but you don't really see your conduct as wrong." I had wanted to disagree, but deep inside knew she was absolutely right. I hated the consequences, but didn't really want to stop. I had not seen lustful thoughts or masturbation as something that grieved God or as something evil. I had enjoyed the false intimacy of fantasy, lust and masturbation, but I had finally reached the point where I knew I needed to die to lust and live for the Lord.

By God's mercy, my wife didn't abandon me. She stood by my side every step of the way. Of course, it took a long time to regain her trust. But for the first time I truly was willing to do whatever it took to stop sinning and start living for purposes greater than my own selfishness. I received Biblical counseling weekly from another Christian man who had been set free from addiction to sex. He started by being open about not being perfect. The safe environment gave me the opportunity to be real—to be myself.

I began to see that my thinking was backward. I saw that my selfishness and pride had fueled my lust. I finally realized that the only hope I had was in turning over all areas of my life to Jesus. I needed to adopt God's plan for living instead of my own. Daily, I spent much time in Bible study and prayer. I began to understand the root sin issues beneath the sexual behavior. I confessed my struggles to a trusted friend, who helped hold me accountable.

I really wanted to be totally free from the bondage of lust and sexual impurity. But more than that, I wanted to return home to God, to live out of love, and to live for Jesus. It was then that I finally began living a victorious life free from the grip of lust and masturbation.

During this process, I began seeing how selfish I had been. I had loved the praise of others. I even thought that somehow God loved me more than others. I finally understood that I was proud and my pride was fighting against the Lord. It was no wonder I was stuck in bondage to masturbation; I was selfish in everything I did. God needed to break my pride before I could truly be free of sexual sin and all the other sins driven by my selfishness.

Each moment you allow Jesus to live through you, you take on humility—the antidote for the pride that feeds your lust. You'll have new desires (God's desires) and experience freedom and joy, even in the midst of trials.[72]

How do you take on His nail-pierced hands? Christ has already told you, before he was crucified: "If anyone desires to come after me, let him deny himself, and take up his cross daily, and follow me."[73] It was Christ's role to pay the punishment for your sin on the cross; it's your role to exchange a worldly life for one hidden in Christ Jesus Himself as you deny yourself and follow Him.

Denying the self is not only an act of humility, but self-denial also happens to be the only place where a real relationship with God can fully prosper. As a created being, you must deny your self-worth while admitting that Jesus is God, then worshiping and trusting Him in all things. Exchanging your hands for Christ's is symbolic of dying to the self and yielding your life completely to Him.

The only way you can hope to stop living for yourself is deciding from this day on, "I will live for Christ." It's a real and permanent commitment each Proven Man must make. It's also the foundation for wanting to live out a Proven life. Your new heart will sing, "I want to reach as high toward the holy mountain as I can and to do whatever it takes to be with God, to experience Him, and receive His healing."

▶ TIM: Finding Acceptance

Tim was only willing to start attending the purity group because he was afraid his wife would leave. Although he had little choice but to attend the next Proven Men session, Tim knew he needed to find out what he was getting into, so he could protect himself. He carefully watched the leader of the group at other church functions. He noticed his every move, his every word to others, so he could understand what kind of a man this was. "Would he be holier-than-thou? Would he be puffed up? Would he be judgmental?" At least from a distance, the man seemed real, open and approachable. Most importantly, he didn't seem to use harsh words. Others seemed to respect him. Maybe it would not be so bad.

Just to be safe, Tim decided to test the leader by only giving him a few details of his secret sin to see how the man would react. When the leader showed him unconditional love, Tim was shocked. At first, he wasn't sure how to take it. His own father had never treated him with such simple, yet complete, acceptance. Tim began to wonder whether the promises in the Bible just might hold true for him. Tim saw the heart of God through the heart of a man and it gave him hope. Maybe, just maybe, he could change his ways. With his marriage on the line, he had no real choice but to risk it all and open his heart to the Lord.

In the months that followed, Tim found that, no matter what secrets he revealed to the leader, he was always met with acceptance and grace. If a man could respond in this way, surely God would be even more accepting.

Another thing Tim didn't expect was that the man leading Proven Men seemed to see right through him and yet he refused to judge or push him away. Instead, he hugged him and told him that he loved him. With such deep, open-hearted acceptance, it was not long before Tim told the man his whole story. A part of him hoped the leader would reject him and run away, as Tim expected. It would have proved he had been right all along. But another, stronger part of him yearned to believe that God's healing was really attainable for him. This man was Tim's litmus test. For the first time, Tim began to believe that God the Father was really a loving Father—a Father he could open his heart to.

Do You Want to be Made Well?

The most common reason why a man doesn't experience lasting freedom from sexual sin is his refusal to embrace the Lord's healing path. He wants to do it his own way. He wants to control life. This concept is contained in the following passage where Jesus addressed a crippled man:

> *Now there is in Jerusalem by the Sheep Gate a pool, which is called in Hebrew, Bethesda, having five porches. In these lay a great multitude of sick people, blind, lame, paralyzed, waiting for the moving of the water. For an angel went down at a certain time into the pool and stirred up the water; then whoever stepped in first, after the stirring of the water, was made well of whatever disease he had. Now a certain man was there who had an infirmity thirty-eight years. When Jesus saw him lying there, and knew that he already had been in that condition a long time, He said to him, "Do you want to be made well?"*

> *The sick man answered Him, "Sir, I have no man to put me into the pool when the water is stirred up; but while I am coming, another steps down before me." Jesus said to him, "Rise, take up your bed and walk." And immediately the man was made well, took up his bed, and walked.*[74]

Think about the interaction here. The crippled man had his own idea of the healing path, which didn't include God. First, the man didn't go to Jesus, but Christ went to Him. Second, even though Jesus had healed numerous crippled people by then, the man didn't inquire about or seek out Jesus to heal him. Rather, it was Christ who initiated the dialogue. Knowing this man's need, Jesus cut right to the heart of the matter by asking the man to decide whether he really wanted to be well.

Did you notice that the man had been hanging around others who were getting well by soaking in the fountain of life, but had never made it in himself? Maybe he enjoyed the pity or perhaps he had gotten so used to his sin that he had forgotten what it was like to become well. Think through the man's response. He was saying that not a single time in thirty-eight years (13,870 days) did he first get into the healing pool. (Did you ever wonder where the phrase "lame excuse" originated?)

One beautiful aspect of the way in which Christ went about freeing the man was that He didn't shame him. Jesus didn't address the excuse at all. No, the Lord was interested in giving him abundant life and full healing.

But was the man ready? Was he finally willing to do it God's way? Notice that Jesus didn't instantly heal him, but told the cripple to do three things to be made well: Get up, pick up your bed, and walk.

These may seem simple to you, but for an invalid, they were impossible. You might also be wondering how picking up a bed forms the basis for a healing path, but it too required three things: Conviction (true desire), faith, and action.

God's design for healing from sexual sins requires no less conviction, faith, and action. First, you must truly want to be well (choosing Christ over anything else in the world). Second, you must trust in His strength instead of your own. Third, you must be a doer, not merely a listener, by acting upon what the Lord reveals (incorporating into your daily life all six elements of a Proven life).

For you, Christ is freely offering healing and lasting freedom, but just as with the lame man, He requires you to come with conviction, faith, and action according to His plan.

Stretching for Freedom

You may not be an invalid sitting next to a healing pool finding excuses for not getting in, but, if you're like most people, you surely have some of your own lame excuses or backward thinking about the healing path to sexual integrity. You also have had your own reasons for refusing conviction, faith, and action.

Let's start from today. If Jesus were asking you whether you really want to be absolutely pure, how would you respond?

▶ STAN: Time to Make a Choice

Stan began to love going to the Proven Men small groups each week. He was no longer in the glass house. It was safe to admit he was not perfect. At first, however, Stan was skeptical of the path. He already knew the Bible. In fact, he had gotten As in his college seminary courses. But he was starting to see how he had been like the Pharisees who knew the Bible without knowing the Lord. The simplicity of the Gospel was breaking his proud heart.

Yet, it wasn't all a bed of roses. Stan had formed a habit of turning to porn as his little treat for being so good. And then there was Missy. Every time he was with her, he burned with passion. It wasn't easy going backward in the physical part of their relationship. Having tasted the sweet water, it was hard not to return for it again. But he wanted to honor Missy. He wanted to start over, to have a second virginity. Equally important, he wanted to be a leader spiritually. Missy's consent to premarital sex didn't make it right. He wanted to be the knight, protecting the fair maiden.

It was good for Stan to listen to the stories of others in the group. The married men spoke of the damage pornography and even premarital sex had done to their marriages, many of which were just hanging on by a thread. It was also good to hear the same struggles among the single men. It was time for Stan to make a choice.

Take a moment to imagine yourself standing next to the Washington Monument. It is 555 feet tall. Can you touch the top? Of course not! Well, imagine that it represents God's standard for holiness or sexual integrity. Will you ever reach it? The truth is, none of us will. But it isn't how tall you stand, but how much you desire holiness and closeness to the Lord that matters.

Because it's impossible to reach the top (to attain absolute purity), most people seem content leaning against God's standard at their own natural height. A second group of men, perhaps most men in church, go a bit further. They lift an arm slightly above their heads so that they are above the first group.

But a Proven Man approaches it differently. He positions his entire body to the wall to allow him to stretch as high as he can. Viewed from a distance, however—from a block away or from an airplane—no one would notice the extra inch he gained, but a Proven Man wants to get as close as he can to God. So he moves closer and stretches as high as he can. Every muscle in his shoulder and side feels the strain as he strives for the extra millimeter. Now he gets up on his toes to really lean into it. He is giving it his all. Even his calves are feeling the stretch. It's hard work.

Although he only moved a tiny bit closer to the Lord, something of great spiritual importance is taking place. If you stretch against the wall this way, you'll notice it too. As you move upward to gain that last millimeter, your head actually points up, lifting your gaze to heaven.

The first group doesn't care. The second group looks around to see where everyone else is on the wall. They snap their heads back and forth to compare themselves to others. They may even take pride in thinking they are higher than many.

In truth, when you're more interested in yourself and your circumstances, you're in the second group; comparing yourself to others and clinging to your rights. That's not God's design or intent. You're not to judge your relationship with the Lord based upon what others are doing.[75] Instead, you're to passionately seek the Lord with all of *your* heart, mind and soul.[76]

Think of your stance on the wall as representative of your pursuit of holiness *because* He is holy. You must keep stretching and reaching out to God. Those in the second group remain stuck in bondage to sexual sin. They want to make just enough effort to feel good about themselves; especially in the eyes of others.

Perhaps you too had been hoping others noticed how pure you were, so you could receive praise or maybe you were content because you were already living more purely than most. Comparing yourself to others merely feeds the false notion that if you don't masturbate or look at pornography as much as before, then you're pure enough. But the goal can never be to reduce or eliminate a sin at the cost of limiting your relationship and intimacy with God.

Making your Decision

Are you willing to do whatever it takes to live in freedom from bondage to sin and to be holy because God is holy? Will you finally agree to give God total and complete control of your life, including your hands, heart, soul, and mind?

If you're willing to make this decision, you'll be free. You don't have to keep feeling defeated by the world. You can live victoriously in the strength of the Lord. Real freedom awaits you!

Right now, make a permanent commitment in your heart to die to self and live for Christ. Don't wait a moment longer.

Chapter 8

Your Game Plan

Can you imagine a professional sport team not scouting out the competition or at least developing a game plan? Of course not! And neither should you when it comes to sexual temptations. You need a separate game plan for each type of situation where temptation has seized you in the past. What about being bored while searching the Internet? Maybe you lust after women at the gym. Perhaps you sometimes order an adult film in your hotel when you travel for work. Let's not forget places such as the shopping mall or, worse yet, the beach.

Each situation requires a game plan for that particular type of temptation because the way of escape looks a bit different. In addition, you don't want to wait until a wave of temptation hits you to start thinking of a way out. You need to make a decision for sexual integrity in advance. This chapter discusses how to recognize and tackle triggers, followed by a section discussing how to include in your game plan the setting of healthy boundaries. As you read these sections, purpose to take the time to develop your own game plans for your triggers and tempting circumstances.

Tackling Triggers

Triggers don't just knock on your mind with a tempting, impure thought but they often lead you to act upon the temptation. Therefore, you need to be mindful of your "triggers" and stop them in their tracks before they turn to action. As I am sure you know, staying pure is a lot easier if you cut off the temptation early. When you wait to take action until you are in the midst of a common trigger, it's generally too late. You've already decided to give in.

A trigger precedes sexual sin. For many men, stress triggers the temptation to turn to pornography or fantasy as an escape (i.e., you soothe yourself with a little reward). Two other common triggers are being alone or having a fight with a loved one. Watching TV, surfing the Internet, or driving past a certain store can all be triggers.

Everyone is different. Take time to identify your own individual triggers. If you become aware of your triggers, you won't be caught off guard. Notice not only what appeals to you as a sexual thought, but also what situations make you more vulnerable to temptation.

If you're committed to sexual integrity, you must be committed to do business with your triggers by planning in advance how you'll respond to them. That means developing a game plan in advance for each one. Yes, that takes time and energy, but what's the cost of allowing the enemy to sneak up on you?

▶ JOEL: Planning for Triggers

I had trained myself to sexualize everything. For instance, I positioned myself to be at the right place to look down a woman's blouse, especially if she may need to bend over. Every time I entered a room, I would know where every woman was and had ranked them in order of beauty. I barely met a pretty woman I didn't include in my fantasies, even some of my friends' wives. In fact, my sinful motto was "staring, glaring, and comparing." There were so many bad behaviors leading to bad inputs that it would take an all out battle to have victory.

I was determined to change and be stamped PROVEN. I would eliminate the bad inputs. For instance, I stared at the ground on my subway commute. I would even stand to the right side and close my left eye when riding up escalators so I would not look at the women walking up the escalator past me. I even gave up watching TV for a year because I tended to lust after women in shows or commercials.

But that wasn't enough. I needed a plan for the triggers, such as when I had a fight with my wife. When we fought, I had often thought to myself, who needs her. I would escape into fantasy through masturbation. I also knew that the shopping mall was a bad place, so I didn't go there for months. I went through the effort of thinking through every trigger and put into place a game plan for each. That's because if I was not prepared for each different setting I knew I would react the way I had trained myself to lust.

An example of a game plan for traveling out of town on business included letting my networking partner know. When I got into the hotel room, I would unplug the TV and place a towel over the screen. That way I needed two steps to turn it on. Also, I brought my Bible study to do and an encouraging book to read at night to *replace* TV. I would also call my wife each evening.

An example of a game plan looks like this:

If you always look at pornography when you are home alone, then plan activities to do when you are alone. Contact your networking partner if you are going to be alone. If he is not available, then call another person from church just to ask them to pray with you.

You don't even need to ask this substitute person to pray about your struggle. Go ahead and pray for missionaries or others in need. The key is to take the focus off yourself and put in onto the Lord.

It's *not* a good game plan to wait until you are home alone to suddenly try thinking of something else to do. Create beforehand a list of healthy things to do when you are alone. Decide beforehand that, if those healthy things fail, you will go out to be around people and less tempting settings. But don't game yourself. Honestly choose a location that will decrease the risk, not simply provide another trigger—such as the gym, the beach or the private corner in an Internet café.

You know yourself. You know what triggers your temptations and what changes need to be made to eliminate the overwhelming sensual inputs.

The more committed you are to sexual integrity, the more you will create a game plan for the common situations where you know you'll be tempted—at work, at home, at the grocery store, when you are bored or tired. Again, each of these may need a different game plan.

Make a firm decision that you won't let triggers control you. It may be that you stop being alone until winning those battles. You might also give up your gym membership, stop watching television, or forgo surfing the Internet for a season. Be willing to do whatever it takes, and be purposed in the battle.

Righting Rituals

You also need to disrupt your rituals, which are slightly different from triggers. A ritual is anything you routinely do as part of the building up process of acting out. You get the point. Rituals are even more dangerous than triggers because rituals are things you plan out in advance as part of the build up to sexual sin. For instance, some men plan to take a shower in the afternoon while others surf the Internet as a prelude to masturbation. For others, rituals involve hanging out at a magazine rack to look at the scanty covers or driving past certain parts of town where women jog.

▶ TIM: Doing Business with Triggers

Tim had many triggers, such as being lonely or bored. The biggest was any time someone said something critical. It brought him back to when his dad told him he was worthless. Tim's reaction would be to hide in fantasy and masturbation.

During one Proven Men meeting, Tim mentioned that when someone says "Hey, Tim," the hairs on his neck stand up and he recoils with fear. His dad had always started with that phrase when criticizing him. To inspire Tim, the Proven Men leader wrote a song that week and sang it to Tim at the next meeting. It was named "Hey, Tim," and each refrain was similar to this: "Hey, Tim, don't you know that I love you; Hey, Tim, I think you are the greatest." Although the music was off tune, it was sweet music for Tim, who wept like a child.

Over time, Tim began believing that the Lord loves him and that God is worthy to be served. Therefore Tim started doing business with his triggers. For instance, he stopped going out to lunch to avoid places where he ate desserts as a prelude and used the restrooms to carry out his action. Now, his plan included talking to his wife about his painful past and his fear of intimacy. In addition, Tim carried with him on a note card his life verse of Romans 8:1 *(there is no condemnation for those in Christ Jesus)*. He would also purpose to reject instead of dwelling on the condemning thoughts that wanted to flood his mind. He would also replace ugly thoughts by looking at a picture of his wife and child and praise the Lord for them.

Tim began taking on new challenges, willing to risk not being perfect. To his amazement, he could lead. He no longer worked for his dad, but bought his own shop. He also took risks by leading at home. His wife was grateful that she didn't have to carry the load by herself anymore.

Right now, identify your rituals, and then make a decision to end these rituals. Let yourself know that they are no longer options. Then do whatever it takes to put them to death. It may mean changing your route to work. Again, it may include giving up your gym membership or not using the computer while alone or at all. Many men become so serious that they give up all television or the Internet for a year and replace them with healthy activities.

Setting Boundaries

You cannot heap burning coals on your lap and not get burned.[77] In other words, you cannot keep playing with temptations without giving in. That's why you need to set some boundaries, which are lines you won't cross or things you won't entertain. You also must be willing to do whatever it takes to not cross them, regardless of how much it costs.

For the single men that know they always go too far on dates, it may require never being alone with your date. You cannot put the cat back in the bag, and for many single men, this is the only sure-fire boundary that will prevent the harm caused by premarital sex. Because single Stan set this boundary of never being alone with Missy, he stopped having premarital sex.

Married men might set a boundary of never being alone with or even discussing personal matters with a woman other than his wife. You may think this sounds crazy, but that's how affairs begin. Because I have a non-negotiable boundary to never be alone with a woman, I can hardly ever have a physical affair, as long as I keep that vow.

But be careful not to rely too heavily on boundaries. Consider the admonition of the Lord:

> *Since you died with Christ to the basic principles of the world, why, as though you still belonged to it, do you submit to its rules: "Don't handle! Don't Taste!"? These are all destined to perish with use, because they are based on human commands and teachings. Such regulations indeed have an appearance of wisdom, with their self-imposed worship, their false humility and their harsh treatment of the body, but they lack any value in restraining sensual indulgences.*[78]

Do you see how rules, such as avoiding certain practices (i.e., don't look or touch), fail to stop the "desire" to do sinful acts? Does this reinforce why setting strict boundaries (i.e., what magazines to read, movies to watch, Internet sites to visit, stores to avoid) won't, by themselves, set you free from lust or addiction to pornography?

In addition, remember the passage which said that sweeping a house clean without filling it simply invites the same sin to revisit in even stronger attacks.[79] That's why "programs" don't work. That's why sexual integrity demands that you set your heart toward God and give up control of your life to Him.

The point is that setting boundaries won't eliminate your desire to lust or to engage in sexual sins. But that doesn't mean you don't set boundaries. They're still an important part of the overall game plan. But the key is to simultaneously pursue a love relationship with God. That's the source of lasting victory because your internal desires begin to conform to God's holy desires. Otherwise, your vacant house will be ripe for other and worse sins to find a home.[80]

▶ STAN: A Game Plan for Triggers

Stan used to love going to the gym. It was included in the price of college tuition. It wasn't clear whether it was a runner's high or sexual fantasy that made the treadmill so enjoyable. He always found a spot near the young ladies and allowed his eyes to enjoy the view of their firm bodies. He also was on the Internet daily, frequently to sites where seductively dressed women were featured, whether it was sporting news or the latest video on Youtube®.

If he made a list of places that fueled fantasy, Stan would add magazine racks, coffee houses, everywhere on college campus, and even church. His list of triggers included being bored and also the stress from juggling his classes, sports and even kissing Missy. The more he thought about it, the more he discovered that he was a budding sex addict.

Stan was not pleased to know how much of a foothold he gave to Satan when it came to fixating on sex in his daily life. He began making a game plan for each of the different places or triggers that enticed him. He knew he needed to do business with each one separately, as each had different attractions and different solutions. For instance, Stan decided not to go to the gym for a season because he couldn't keep his eyes from wandering. That place was just too great a temptation. He also put filters on his computer and never used the computer when he was alone. He would go to the school library to use it. While in the library, he also chose a desk that faced the wall, instead of ones where the ladies walked past.

The final frontier was what to do about Missy. This would prove to be his biggest challenge. His leader suggested that he make the hard choice of never being alone with Missy in his apartment or other places where they used to make out. Was that too radical? Was it truly necessary?

Sacking Setbacks

There's no one who is perfect or without sin. Even after you chart a course of earnestly seeking the Lord and striving for absolute purity, you'll probably experience moments of failures and setbacks. Please hear me; you are not abnormal if you have a setback. We all do at times.

When you have setbacks, it's time to stand on God's promise that He renews and restores: "He who was seated on the throne said, 'I am making everything new!'"[81] Indeed, "our great God and Savior, Jesus Christ, ... gave himself for us to redeem us from all wickedness and to purify for himself a people that are his very own, eager to do what is good."[82]

Although God doesn't grant a license to sin, He instructs you how to respond when you stumbled in order to be fully restored. That's right. The Lord won't reject you, but tells you what to do when you have a setback.

Not sure that this applies to you, that God will still treat you as a dearly loved child if you have a setback? Well, you're not a special case, so stop beating yourself up if you have a setback. Otherwise you play right into the hands of the devil that wants you to hide from, not turn to, Jesus.

Consider Apostle Peter. He was the right hand man of Jesus. Although we aren't told of any sexually related setbacks, we know Peter had plenty of setbacks. They each occurred when Peter took his eyes off of the Lord. That's the same thing that leads up to a sexual setback. Peter's setbacks are worthy of notice because all setbacks involve the same cure, putting your eyes back on Jesus and striving to live a Proven life.

When Jesus was walking on water approaching the boat, Peter was afraid. But that was not the setback. Peter actually walked out on the water to meet Him.[83] But then Peter took his eyes off Jesus and that's when he began to sink.

That's the same way we sink into sexual impurity—taking our eyes off of Jesus.

Peter's next setback happened when he tried to dissuade Jesus from willingly agreeing to suffer and be killed.[84] Peter pushed aside an eternal perspective and wanted Jesus to set up an earthly kingdom right then. It was in response to this setback that Jesus chose to reveal the famous cure we all need: "Whoever wants to be my disciple must deny themselves and take up their cross and follow me."[85]

This is the same cure for sexual setbacks. This is the same Proven Path you must take.

The most famous setback occurred when Peter denied three times even knowing Jesus.[86] But even with that so-called *serious setback*, Jesus restored Peter and invited him to become one of the greatest examples of a Proven Man for generations to come.

Jesus invites you to join Peter's line of disciples willing to pick up the cross and follow Christ, including after each setback.

The other twelve disciples also had setbacks, just like you and I do. It isn't the absence of setbacks that stamps a man PROVEN—it's how he responds.

Consider the sharp contrast of how Judas responded to a setback, compared to Peter.

We know Judas didn't really believe in Jesus. Some think that perhaps one of the reasons Judas betrayed Jesus for thirty silver coins was his attempt to force Jesus to set up a kingdom on earth.[87]

Either way, Judas thought he would make out. If Jesus were to set up his kingdom now, being one of the twelve, well, that would gain him a great position. But, if he was not God, then why follow him and why not get some payment for three years of lost time and wages?

Whatever the plan, it backfired. When Judas realized Jesus was to be killed, he was seized with remorse. But rather than repent and put his eyes on Jesus, Judas committed suicide.[88]

Peter was a Proven Man because of how he responded to setbacks. He quickly put his hope and faith back in the Lord after each setback. No, Peter was not sinless. But yes, he has pretty cool testimonies or stories to tell about being redeemed by Christ. How about the time he walked on water with the Lord? Okay, only a few steps, but he walked on water while he looked to Jesus. How about the number of men he has mentored and networked with in the name of Christ and taught them how about how to pick up their cross and live a victorious life?

Judas, on the other hand, threw in the towel. He couldn't accept that Jesus unconditionally loved him. Judas needed to "earn" God's love. He refused to believe that Jesus forgives every sin that we confess. Sadly, Judas was too proud to ask for forgiveness. Judas was not a Proven Man because he didn't embrace all six elements of a Proven life. If he had repented, he would have been forgiven even for betraying the Lord. There is no sin that is unforgivable, except one: Refusing to believe in Jesus. Even then, the Lord is patient and gives us each day a new today to turn to Him.

Failures often occur when you slip back into old routines. Perhaps you had an argument with someone or are tired or lonely and you let your guard down. Instead of turning immediately to God, old patterns return and trigger a relapse.

Some people even stumble when they get frustrated over the length of time it seems to be taking to be free and they "help" God out. Their efforts fail, because it actually takes back permission for the Lord to work in their lives. God won't force Himself on you and He won't make you live a pure or holy life. Instead, He waits until you grasp that He alone heals and transforms. He waits until you turn to Him. He does this for your good. If the Lord allowed your effort to succeed, you would be puffed up and keep seeking independence. Such rebellion leads only further into the deceitfulness of the world and traps you in bondage to all kinds of sin stemming from selfishness.

Have faith. Be on guard. But don't ever give up. Yes, self-condemnation often follows failure. You feel like throwing in the towel, but God wants to forgive and renew you. So let Him.

One of the first steps in the Proven Path in response to setbacks, whether it's a sexual or other pride-based sin, is to put on an *eternal perspective*. God is in a lifelong process of healing you, changing you, and preparing you for intimacy both now and in heaven. Perhaps the most important understanding you can have is that the Lord loves you unconditionally. That's right, you cannot earn[89] or lose[90] God's great love for you.

It's this complete and available love that draws men to Christ. Will you open the eyes of your soul to the Lord and permit His love to penetrate your heart? In order to position yourself to receive God and experience His love and freedom, you must seek the Lord and truly yield your life to Him. This requires resolution of will to put the Lord first.

Living out a *victorious* life doesn't just happen. It may take longer than you hope or expect for healing to occur. Remember, change is hard. It involves a battle. It requires more than your own will; you must have God-sized strength.

When you have setbacks (and you will), stand on God's promise that He renews and restores: "He who was seated on the throne said, 'I am making everything new!'"[91] Indeed, "our great God and Savior, Jesus Christ … gave himself for us to redeem us from all wickedness and to purify for Himself a people that are his very own, eager to do what is good."[92]

Many Proven Men small group leaders have confessed their setbacks to me. I first affirm them—gently speaking my love and respect. I also instruct them that, as a leader, they face heightened temptations and spiritual attacks. They need to be on guard 24/7, as Satan knows that an attack on them also weakens the men they lead. Next, I encourage them to reexamine their game plan and ensure it includes talking to their regular *networking partner* before, during, and after a setback. Finally, I remind them that, just as the Lord is faithful to forgive, they are forgiven and restored by accepting His grace of repentance. I highlight that they are still Proven Men and are able to lead small groups. (There are times, of course, when a small group leader who is riding a roller coaster may need to take a season from leading a group in order to concentrate on firming up all six elements of the PROVEN acronym in his life.)

As far as the men's progress in Proven Men support groups, one of my greatest joys is listening to them describe what they learned about themselves or about the Lord after a setback. Rather than remain stuck or wallow in shame, the Spirit empowers them to focus on moving forward. Frequently, the stories consist of how God opened certain areas of their life or heart that were once closed off because of their selfishness and pride. Other stories include how they were able to repent of sin or praise the Lord in ways they never knew or thought possible. It is at those moments that I joyfully remind myself: **The measure of a *Proven Man* is not the absence of sin, but how a man responds to a setback.** In fact, take on the *eternal perspective* that a setback is an opportunity to learn from and lean upon God.

Listening to the Wrong Voice

The battle for purity actually takes place in the spirit world. Spiritual warfare is real. If you're not engaged in it, you can expect to experience regular setbacks.

If you were playing a new game with someone and you didn't bother to read the rules, you would incur a lot of fouls and miss out on a lot of opportunities. Well, how will you know how to fight or win a spiritual war if you choose to ignore it?

One reason men remain stuck in bondage to sexual sin is that they are listening to the wrong voice. The one they hear says, "You've already sinned, so you might as well throw in the towel." For instance, after Bart clicks on a website link that leads him to a pornography page, he feels unworthy and decides he might as well look at it. After feeling even more guilt over looking so long, he figures he sinned already, so he may as well masturbate. Then he hides from God, much like Judas, incorrectly thinking his sin is too great for God to forgive.

The problem is that Bart was listening to the wrong voice. He hadn't previously taken seriously the spiritual battle; therefore, he hadn't learned to tell the difference between the voices of God—who wanted him to succeed—and that of the devil—who wanted him to be shamed and turn to himself (or the world) instead of God.

Here's how you can tell the difference.

The voice of the Lord is always gently calling you to His home. He isn't forceful or hurried, but soft. However, the voice of Satan is rushed, loud and immediate. You feel pressured to quickly act and end up rushing to strive in your own strength.

Consider the difference between two parents teaching a child to ride a bike.[93] The first one is gentle. He tells his son how much he loves him. He tells him not to be afraid as he removes the training wheels. "I'll be right here with you." He holds the bike as the child gets on. He trots slowly by him giving encouraging instructions. "That's right. You are doing great. Keep peddling."

The second parent is rushed. "I only have a few minutes, so you better be ready to ride this bike. I took off the sissy wheels. It should only take one try, unless you are a dope." When the child tips and falls, the first father is nurturing. "I fell many times when I learned to ride. I think I still have a scar on my leg. Wow, you did so well! I can see that you will be a great rider." The second parent tells the child, "I knew you would fail." He then proceeds to point out that he spent long hours at work to be able to buy the bike. He is demeaning and makes the child feel unworthy of the time spent. The child thinks his dad cares more for things than him.

Are you getting the picture? God is a gentle loving Father. He is patient and kind, offering grace and encouragement. On the other hand, Satan is condemning, rushed and loud. He wants you to chase instant pleasures and to feel bad about yourself. All Satan really cares about is that you don't turn to the Lord. The more the devil can convince you to look to yourself (your circumstances, rights or needs) the easier he can get you to look to the world for fixes.

When you have a failure, such as looking at porn, God remains kind and forgiving. He gently encourages you to return to Him right away. Satan would have you believe you're no good and not worth the bother to God. The devil feeds the feeling, "I may as well give over completely to sin."

Will you slow down and listen to God? Will you draw close to hear His gentle voice? Reject Satan's lies. Get to know your loving Father by immersing yourself in His truth (the Bible), spending daily time in worship of the only truly perfect being, and talking openly to the Lord as a friend. That's why there are six elements to a Proven life. Each one brings you closer to God.

The more you incorporate all six aspects of the PROVEN acronym into each day, the easier it will be to hear and discern God's voice and know that you're truly forgiven and deeply loved. You'll also begin to recognize when Satan is trying to tear you down with lies to steer you toward any road leading away from God.

Embrace the *PROVEN* Path

Stop trying in your own efforts. Make a permanent decision to trust God no matter what the circumstances. You'll be riding your bike again in no time, carried along by your loving Father. The Lord will pick you up when you fall and will fully restore you. Turn to and completely trust God. Always remember that God wants to forgive and restore you. But you need to repent by asking for forgiveness and wanting to return under His wing.

Ultimately, putting into practice a daily life of incorporating each of the six letters of the PROVEN acronym is ultimately what you need to sack setbacks. Here they are again:

Passionate for God,
Repentant in spirit,
Open and honest,
Victorious in living,
Eternal in perspective, and
Networked with other *Proven Men.*

As you focus on including these things in your daily life, instead of fixating on your circumstances, you'll be putting on the armor of God and will properly respond to setbacks. Therefore, purpose to not only memorize the PROVEN letters but test your life daily against them.

Following is a quick review of the importance of each letter.

Passion for God. Without passion for God, your soul will never find freedom and receive healing. It begins with humility—knowing in your inner being that the Lord is the One who created you and that apart from Him, you can do nothing. Deep love and thanksgiving will pour out from you as you begin experiencing His great love.

Repentant in Spirit. Pride is the greatest barrier to knowing and experiencing God. It also blocks out intimate relationships with others. True repentance lays down self-interest and rights. It allows you to freely forgive. In humility, you realize that your greatest sin is departing from God as you go your own way to carry out your selfish desires. With repentance, you race back to the Lord to be near Him again.

Openness in Communication with God and Others. Talk to the Lord as a friend, telling Him of your struggles and listening when He speaks. Purpose to build relationships with others too! By allowing yourself to have feelings, which are intended for your good, you will be able to feel it sooner if you begin to stray from your close connection with the Lord.

Victorious Living Under His Authority. Each moment you live by the Spirit, you'll be able to master each desire that enters your mind (Galatians 5:16). God wants you to draw near to Him so He can give you His righteousness and power to live in holiness and be united with Him in spirit. Stop striving with your own strength and receive the Lord Himself so you can be transformed.

Eternal in Perspective. As you look for meaning beyond your own circumstances, your world expands, enabling you to take an interest in others and conquer the sin of selfishness. The more clearly you understand that your home is in heaven, the more your work on earth will take on new meaning. You can look to and rely upon the Lord for strength to fulfill your purpose in life. You'll no longer need to control your life, but will gladly submit your will to the Lord and ask Him to carry out His plan as you seek after Him with all your heart.

Need of (Networking with) Others. You'll never be stamped PROVEN by standing alone. The Lord uses others in your life to encourage you and offers you a chance to encourage them in return. Work to develop your relationships (network) with other men who are diligently seeking the Lord and who, just like you, are finished with pretending or trying to go it alone.

PART III

THE PRACTICE

Passionate for God,

Repentant in spirit,

Open and honest,

Victorious in living,

Eternal in perspective, and

Networking with other *Proven Men.*

Chapter

Put Down the Shovel and Pick Up the Sword

Most men like being given lists of things to do so they can attack the problem and measure the results. That's what makes a step program to sexual healing sound so appealing.

Okay. Ask yourself this: If there were a list of things you could do that would guarantee you would never commit a sexual sin, would you do it? The Bible does provide exactly such a list—eight things that will keep you from falling:

> *But also for this very reason, giving all diligence, add to your faith virtue, to virtue knowledge, to knowledge self-control, to self-control perseverance, to persever- ance godliness, to godliness brotherly kindness, and to brotherly kindness love. For if these things are yours and abound, you will be neither barren nor unfruitful in the knowledge of our Lord Jesus Christ. For he who lacks these things is shortsighted, even to blindness, and has forgotten that he was cleansed from his old sins.*

Therefore, brethren, be even more diligent to make your call and election sure, for if you do these things you will never stumble....[94]

There you have it. The remedy for never backsliding is living out faith, virtue, knowledge, self-control, perseverance, godliness, brotherly kindness, and love.

Now that you have been given the answer—the eight things that will ensure that you'll never stumble—consider how hard it will be to live out a single one of these things, let alone all eight!

To make matters worse, the Lord says that each of these qualities must be "yours and abound," which means you must possess them in greater abundance and in ever-increasing measure. In other words, you must constantly and forever be pursuing these things with all of your heart with ever *increasing* devotion.

You can easily see that, as you attempt to reach this holy standard, you will fail. You'll be weighed down beyond what you can bear—*if you try to do it with your own strength.*

In fact, God warns that in your own power you won't succeed.[95] It's time to agree with God that, apart from Him, you can do nothing of eternal value.[96] That's why you must live by the Holy Spirit instead of relying upon your own strength.[97]

Are you ready to stop relying upon self-effort and give total control to God? The Lord assures us that, "My yoke is easy and my burden is light."[98] His precious promises apply equally to the list of eight things. Examine more closely what God has to say about equipping you for living out these eight things:

His divine power has given to us all things that pertain to life and godliness, through the knowledge of Him who called us by glory and virtue, as His divine power has

given to us all things that pertain to life and godliness,
through the knowledge of Him who called us by glory
and virtue, by which have been given to us exceedingly
great and precious promises, that through these you may
be partakers of the divine nature, having escaped the
corruption that's in the world through lust.[99]

God knows that His children want to escape the corruption in the world and to overcome their own evil desires. Yet, He also knows that you need His power to live in victory. That's why, before He gave you a list of eight virtues that will keep you from turning to lust and sexually immoral practices, Jesus made it clear that *He* is the source of promises, *He* is the source of the power to overcome the lust of the world, and that *He* is making *His* power available!

Never forget that God wants you to succeed. Remember, He made you in His image for the wonderful opportunity of becoming an adopted son and best friend.

Think of the above passage as a pep talk before the big game. Perhaps the coach says it this way:

Okay, son. Don't forget, you are on my team. No one has
more power or weapons than us. I gave you the playbook
and all of the equipment. You even carry my name on
your jersey. If you stick to the game plan, you will win.
You've sat the bench long enough and I want you to be
a starter. I have full confidence in you!

God's Word is encouraging, but if you stop with pep talk alone, you won't succeed. You need more than emotion. You need more than your own efforts. That's why even completing a 12-week study or following the latest program won't keep you from returning to your sin. You must undergo an exchanged life. That means daily living out all six elements of a Proven life from a heart that wants to know and rely upon God.

In order to continue to possess the very things your soul and heart cries out for (i.e., faith, goodness, knowledge, self-control, perseverance, godliness, brotherly kindness, or love), you must keep growing in your knowledge of Christ forever. Those who daily live by the Spirit of God receive His strength and victory, but those that treat the Proven Path as a magic formula or temporary fix will return to their same detestable sins as a dog returns to its own vomit.[100]

Isn't it wonderful how all Scripture is intertwined! Before asking you to incorporate into your life eight principles needed to live victoriously, God reminds you that He gives you His power and strength and knowledge and wisdom and glory and goodness and promises. True freedom rings when you participate with God in clothing yourself with these eternal qualities that set you free from the evil desires that had constantly dragged you down. Simply put, the Lord offers you His very divine nature so that you can be renewed and transformed, stamped PROVEN and escape the corruption of the world.

If you're still relying upon your talent, your resolve, a set of rules, or some other idea for quenching lust, you won't ever find freedom. Instead, God has a radical two-part solution:
- *die completely to self,* and
- *live wholly for Christ.*[101]

The Shovel of Self-Effort

In taking on the power of Christ, you must stop striving with your own strength. But it cannot end there. Living for the Lord means giving Him preeminent control of your heart, soul, mind, and body.

Imagine that you were given a shovel when you were born. You use the shovel to dig. Only one person can use the shovel at a time. While you're digging, God watches. He waits for you to put the shovel down, in order to pick it up and use His wisdom and strength to build your life. The biggest problem you face is a lack of faith that if you set the shovel down that Jesus will pick it up and complete the project. You imagine the shovel sitting there doing nothing. Perhaps, instead, you are afraid God will want to do a different project than the one you want to do. Therefore, you keep a tight hold of the shovel and dig like crazy. The moments you put the shovel down to rest, God doesn't pick it up because you lack faith that He will do the job "correctly." You simply refuse to turn the project over to Him.

Just as with the fear of putting down the shovel of self-effort, when temptation to lust surfaces you're afraid that it will overtake you if you simply trust in God. So you keep trying in vain by using your own strength. You put more trust in Internet filters and setting man-made boundaries than you do in setting aside time to meet with the Lord and in giving Him control of your life. The problem is that when acting in your own strength, the battle will get too hard and you'll eventually give in.

But God says you can trust in Him to overcome.[102] Christ will pick you up and give you His strength.[103] He will not lead you into, but through temptation.[104]

▶ **JOEL: Done Pretending**

Initially, I was only pretending that I wanted to stop lust and masturbation. I had given Christ every part of my heart, well all except this one small, tiny little place. It was so small that it would not show up on an X-ray machine. I had convinced myself that God would overlook it when compared to how much else I did for God. The times when I cried out to the Lord to take away the temptation, I was really only interested in ridding myself of guilt. I thought I couldn't live without the nightly escape into fantasy.

It wasn't until my marriage was on the line that I had to make a choice between the real woman God provided to me and the fake ones I created. I had to answer the question, "Do I want to get well?" Now, for the first time, I really could say yes. I was finally willing to go through life relying on the Lord instead of the temporary relief of masturbation. I was determined to have conviction, faith, and action. No more games. No more secret lives.

The shovel analogy also really struck home. I was the classic man who believed, "I can do it myself." In fact, my dad had raised me to live by the motto: "If I can't do it myself, I don't need it." My father taught me that it was a sign of weakness to ask anyone for help.

Finally, I understood why the Lord had allowed one thing to remain in my life that was too big for me. If I didn't have to rely upon the Lord for purity, I would have been puffed up with pride claiming I beat it on my own. I would have kept living my life on my own for my own. But that's not God's way. The Lord opposes the proud, but gives grace to the humble. I finally chose to humble myself and stop fighting against God.

Although frightened to be out of control, I was going to put down the shovel of self-effort and become a servant of God. I would turn to the Lord for strength and rely on God. That meant rising each day to meet with God and start listening to His voice. I would ask the Lord to be the pilot to purity. I would start doing things God's way.

God has a blueprint and power that far exceeds your ideas and efforts. In fact, the spot you choose to dig always becomes a sand trap. No matter how hard you try, it keeps filling back in. You're not much further now than you were a year ago. The good news is that the Lord wants to be your Master Builder, the One who supplies the materials and ability to build a real oasis. Christ wants you to put the shovel down and believe He will pick it up. You can and must give the Lord total control over all areas of your heart and all aspects of your thought life.

As with the shovel, only one at a time can lead in the fight for integrity—you or God. When you put down the shovel of self-effort and give the Lord permission over your life, you won't be lusting for things outside of His kingdom—guaranteed.

Won't you enter the exchanged life and agree to stop trying in your own strength? Begin right now by putting the shovel down and trusting God to pick it up. Ask Him to pick it up for you. Jesus wants to direct your life. He proved His love and worth on the cross.[105] Don't try to take back control again now, no matter how hard it seems. God's plan will work. Five years from now you won't still be up to your ankles in sand, but you'll be living in His oasis.

Now, don't misunderstand: *This doesn't mean that you should sit back and do nothing.* Remember that you still have a striving role, but only to act according to His plan using His spiritual weapons. It's only when you're living moment by moment in the power of God that you enjoy victory over the selfish nature.[106]

Of course, at first, it will be a daily battle to stop trying to control life and a fight to keep from escaping into fantasy. No matter how hard it seems, don't quit. Keep following the Proven Path. Keep relying upon His strength. Keep putting into place all six elements of the PROVEN acronym. As you do, over time you'll find that it's not such a burden to live a Proven life. In fact, as you begin loving the Lord with all you heart, mind and soul, you'll naturally want to do what God wants. It will no longer be about giving up things, but choosing new and wonderful things He has in store for you.

Let's be practical for a moment. This level of surrender to God means you cannot keep secret sins (i.e., picking up your own shovel to dig your own hole when you think no one is watching) and expect God to keep building your oasis as though He were fooled by your double mindedness. You must remove your former way of thinking and exchange it for God's perspective and will. You must be fully devoted to and living in complete reliance upon God. Only then can you bask in the oasis Christ builds, and only then will you be able to be joyful always, praying continually, and thankful in all circumstances.[107]

Remember, it's only by yielding 100 percent to God that you can accomplish the eight things listed earlier and be kept *by Christ* from stumbling.

Commit right now to trusting God with every area of your life.

Seeing God as Good

One reason it's so hard to put down the shovel of self-effort is that you likely don't fully trust God. I know that's a pretty hard statement, but it's true.

Oswald Chambers once said, "The core of all sin is the belief that God is not good."

If you're not passionate about the Lord and striving for absolute purity it's likely because you're internally withholding part of yourself from God. You're holding back because you doubt God is trustworthy. You might think God is too busy to think about you or your situation. If that's the case, then the root issue is that you don't believe that God is good. Others think that they are good themselves. It can be hard to see God as good when you compare Him to yourself!

Let this concept sink in a moment.

You must start seeing God as good in order to put down the shovel. You must see God as good to release the worship that wells up in your soul or to trust Him with the reigns of your life. When you start seeing God as He is—good, perfect and holy—your inward passion to praise Him will be awakened and your trust in Him secure.

The solution to your deadness lies not in merely mouthing praise songs or trying to force worship to work, but in finding and experiencing God one-on-one. Perhaps you don't understand how much difference this can make because you don't really know God. Perhaps you don't go to Him daily, sharing what's on your heart, including your worries, hopes, dreams, and struggles. In some ways, you might have been living only for yourself.

Just as the core of sin is refusing to see God as good, the crux to victory begins by accepting that God alone can fulfill your innate needs. If you fully embrace this, the need to escape into fantasy or false intimacy proportionally lessens.

Because God is perfectly good, your need to passionately worship Him is greater than any clapping or standing ovations you ever gave to another. His perfection is great enough to demand that you love and praise Him with all of your heart, mind, body, and soul. Don't fight it.

The beauty of the way that God designed you is that in direct proportion to the amount of passion you release toward God, your heart and soul are filled with the fruit of His Spirit and its accompanying joy.[108] You have no idea what love, joy, peace, patience, kindness, goodness, faithfulness, gentleness and self-control await you—if you only die to self. Hallelujah, praise the Lord!

Put Down the Shovel, Pick Up the Sword

God created men with a natural desire to impact his world. Some of man's first tasks were to take care of the animals and work the land. You have the same work drive today. That's why it's so hard to put down the shovel of self-effort. You were born to accomplish tasks. The good news is that there are some *actions* involved in living out a Proven life, despite not striving to control life.

Assume you're huddled in a cave. It's dark and misty. Outside are fierce dragons. You hear their high-pitched screeches and the eerie screams of their victims. You're stricken with fear. Yet you know that if you stay hidden in the cave, others who need your help will be killed. A bright light suddenly appears as a mighty warrior clad in golden armor and a sharp sword enters. He looks you in the eyes and says,

> *I am the King of Kings, Prince of Peace, Deliverer, Master, and Redeemer. I am entering into battle with the dragons. I invite you to join me. I have everything you need to be victorious. I have a suit of armor specially designed for you. The dragons cannot penetrate your armor. You cannot suffer a life-threatening blow or injury. I also have a sword for you more powerful than their weapons. Here is my promise to you. Victory is assured if you simply wear your armor, use the sword, and follow me. Will you go with me?*

This is a dream come true. Who wouldn't want to join that battle? You're guaranteed victory. You're assured you won't suffer a mortal wound. Yes, you may suffer some minor scrapes and bruises, but you are slaying dragons ... you are saving the princess! You're living large—the way God designed it for you.

Living out a Proven life means putting down the shovel of self-effort, but it also means putting on the armor of God, including—get this men—*picking up the sword of the spirit.*[109] That's right, you can strive and strain, you can work hard toward a heavenly goal. Proven Men are not lazy or weak, but are fully armed soldiers protecting lives—yours and others.

Here are the key pieces of your spiritual armor:

- the belt of truth
- the breastplate of righteousness
- the Gospel of peace
- the shield of faith
- the helmet of salvation
- the sword of the spirit (Word of God)
- the words of prayer

▶ JOEL: Swinging the Sword with a Soft Heart

The process wasn't easy. I was a man of action. I wanted to fight temptation and defeat the enemy of lust. Therefore, it was hard for me to hear that I needed to put down the shovel of self-effort. I agreed.

As soon as I humbled myself before the Lord, it was exciting to learn that God did want me to participate in the battle. The Lord had a sword for me to use. I was also given other armor to wear during the battle. This time, however, I would follow God. I would begin meeting with the Lord each morning, not to check off homework, but to get to know Him. I wanted a soft heart, to be humble, to follow God's way.

Part of picking up the sword was to recognize that lust and pornography are evil, and attack them as a doctor attacks cancer. I would eradicate the worldly influences and build my life around Godly pursuits. I didn't just want to leave a vacant house behind, but to fill it with the Lord. I gradually became fully committed to sexual integrity. I was going to fight using God's weapons, including memorizing weekly verses. I would stand firm, and rely on the Lord through every temptation.

God's Weapons of War

Victory over sexual sin requires the power of God. It's a spiritual battle. Have you taken upon yourself the spiritual weapons of God? He lays them out for you each day and has given you an instructional manual on using them.[110] When entering a gladiator battle, who wouldn't examine his armor and hone his skills with the sword? The power God offers is spiritual armor you need to defeat any spiritual attack:

- *The Belt of Truth.* Stand firm in the truth of God (the Bible). Know it, believe it, embrace it, and use it. The belt of truth holds the other weapons firmly in place.

- *The Breastplate of Righteousness.* Guard your heart, especially from the lie of self-condemnation and the lusts of the world. Godly protection of the heart, instead of the false façade of being closed and sheltered, enables you to openly communicate and engage in real relationships. A passionate heart also releases praise to the Lord.

- *The Gospel of Peace.* Wearing God's shoes allows you to run toward peace. The right stride is in the humble footsteps of the Lord, where forgiveness is freely granted and where love is not withheld. You also keep your entire body in shape through disciplined training in spiritual warfare.

- *The Shield of Faith.* Satan's fiery darts of fear and doubt are quickly extinguished when you hold the shield of faith soaked daily in God's Word. Actively build up and rely upon your faith in the Commander-in-Chief through daily interaction with God and study of His Word.

- *The Helmet of Salvation.* While the seed of sin starts in the heart, it's carried out in your mind. If you don't take captive every idle thought and make it obedient to Christ, you're giving up valuable ground to the enemy. If you don't kill impure thoughts in their tracks, they will become your master. Uncontrolled thoughts become actions, and actions become habits. Undisciplined thinking will keep you in bondage to lust, greed, worry, doubts and twisted doctrines. Listen to the voice of the Lord, and replace your thoughts with His. Think on things that are pure, lovely and admirable.

- *The Sword of the Spirit (The Word of God).* You can take the offensive and regain lost ground. God has given you weapons far superior to any of Satan's. Use God's spiritual sword, which is active and alive.[111] Grab hold of appropriate Scriptures and allow God to fight for you. Keep your memory verses handy, for the battle is at hand.

- ***The Words of Prayer.*** God answers real prayers. Selfish requests are not prayers at all. Pray according to God's will, especially for others. The condition of your heart and motive is key. When you engage God in true prayer, the floodgates of heaven are opened. The place of power is on your knees in submission to God and reverently seeking His perfect will.

Never forget that each moment you live by the Spirit, you live in victory.[112] Although you must put down the shovel of self-effort, you'll need to work daily at putting on the armor of God, including picking up the sword. You can never be too prepared for battle. It must become second nature.

▶ **STAN: Sacred Sacrifice**

Stan had known sacrifice. He had watched his pastor dad work 70 hours a week, sacrificing everything and receiving little in return. Stan was committed not to making the same mistake. Therefore, Stan was always on guard. He doubted everyone's motive. They only wanted something. At most, Stan was willing to risk his time, but not his heart in helping others.

Then along came Missy. He wanted her in his life. His goal was to marry her. He would win her on his own. Things had been great, until she started backing away due to her guilt over pre-marital sex. First, Stan tried to convince her it was okay, but that didn't work. Next, he relied upon his strength to fight temptation on their dates. It was a battle he couldn't win.

Although Stan couldn't see it at the time, losing the battle for purity was what it took to realize that he was a control freak. It was that need for control that kept God at a distance. Without enlisting God, Stan would not be pure. But God would not act as a vending machine. He didn't answer the purported prayers of Stan asking God to take away the temptations. The Lord was not interested in Stan just refraining from premarital sex, but wanted a real relationship with him. The good news is that Stan started seeing this himself. He was finally willing to open up to the Lord. He was willing to put down the shovel of self-effort.

Swinging the Sword for Absolute Purity

As you might expect from a young man in love, about the only thing on Stan's mind was marrying Missy. Of course, he had wanted some of those benefits now. Fortunately, Stan now realized that building a strong marriage begins while dating. He needed to protect Missy and protect his own sexual integrity.

As hard as it was for Stan to understand, he listened as married men in the group told him that their wives regretted premarital sex after they got married. They carried guilt forward into marriage and it often affected their sexual relations in marriage. Stan also listened as they shared that they too were not immune to the effects of pornography and fantasy. They warned Stan that he was training himself to compare Missy to all the fantasies he allowed in his mind. Each of them was competing against Missy. Stan didn't want to subconsciously compare them to her. Stan didn't want to usher into his marriage the typical male view that sexual relations with a spouse is just "sex," knowing that Missy would be longing for intimacy. In short, Stan knew he needed to swing the sword of the Spirit to fight for purity or he would put his future marriage at risk.

It's essential that you put down the shovel of self-effort and stop acting in your own strength for your own purposes. It's time to yield 100 percent to the Lord. Stop clinging to the world. It won't satisfy. Start trusting God. You can begin by truly believing that God is good.

Once you decide to join God's team by giving up the notion that you must be the boss of your life, you'll be able to pick up the sword of the Spirit. When you rely only upon His strength, you'll be victorious.

▶ TIM: Self-Effort: Who Me?

In his own mind, Tim couldn't do anything right, so it was not hard for him to believe that he needed to put down the shovel of self-effort. But actually Tim was holding just as tight a grip on the shovel as Joel. Tim was committed to control. He desperately needed to control his relationships in order to control the pain. Tim had learned not to trust anyone. He carefully chose what entered his life. He rarely tried anything new and relied on no one, not even God. In fact, Tim was fearful that if he gave God control, the Lord would send him to India to be a missionary. Tim was definitely afraid to give God control.

If Tim couldn't learn to trust God, he couldn't stop striving in his own strength. Because the Lord wanted to bring healing to Tim, he sent a man into his life who would not judge; someone to show unconditional love. The outpouring of grace through a man caused Tim to see God as a loving father for the first time. It gave Tim hope. Tim now realized he could trust the Lord. The more Tim trusted God, the more his heart melted. He began having feelings. He began being open and honest.

Pick Up the Sword: Huh?

In a choice between fight or flight, Tim inevitably chooses flight. He always ran away from confrontation. During high school Tim was the largest kid in school, wearing size 14 shoes that supported his 300 pounds. The football coach made Tim join the team. The problem was that Tim didn't want to hit anyone with his pads. The coach tried to change that through a special session where the coach's kid, who was 150 pounds lighter, was told to keep running at Tim to try to knock him out. Tim easily shoved him away with his hands on every try. When the coach began berating his son for being weak, it was Tim who ran off crying. Tim never put on the pads again.

Tim's fear of confrontation and rejection also affected his marriage. He refused to lead his wife at home or make any decisions, even which restaurant to go to or where to park the car. He didn't want to make yet another mistake. Therefore he didn't have any practice engaging in a battle. It would take everything in him to be willing to stand beside the Lord and fight for purity. Fortunately, his Proven Men leader was patient. He spent time getting to know and encourage Tim. For instance, he suggested that Tim take on Romans 8:1 as his life verse: "Therefore, there is now no condemnation for those who are in Christ Jesus." Tim grew to trust in God's power and to believe He is good. He was now willing to pick up the sword God had for him.

The next chapter teaches you how to begin tackling temptations with the help of the Lord.

Passionate for God,
Repentant in spirit,
Open and honest,
Victorious in living,
Eternal in perspective, and
Networking with other *Proven Men.*

The 3 Rs for Tackling Temptation

Flee—Don't Flirt with—Temptation

Every man is tempted to lust. It's very tempting to indulge in sensual sins—second glances, flirting, undressing women with your eyes.

The Bible speaks of a prostitute sitting at her door inviting men into her house.[113] It says this about those who listen to and join her:

> *Stolen water is sweet; and food eaten in secret is delicious! But little do they know that the dead are there, that her guests are in the depths of the grave.*

Don't be deceived into thinking that these Proverbs only apply to others. There's always a consequence to sin. You're no exception. "Can a man scoop fire into his lap without his clothes being burned?"[114]

Do pornography and other sexual sins still seem delicious to you? God says that those who continue to eat of forbidden fruit are blind and deceived; they'll suffer His wrath. In fact, to love the things of the world is to reject and even hate God.[115] If you don't see that chasing after the things of the world and its passions and pleasures leads to separation from God and if you don't choose to hate pornography and other sins, then you'll face the destruction that flows from sexual immorality. You'll also miss out on the joy and blessings of God.

God knows you're tempted. So, listen to His command and advice: "Flee from sexual immorality."[116]

The Lord explains why this is so important:

> *All other sins a man commits are outside his body, but he who sins sexually sins against his own body. Do you not know that your body is a temple of the Holy Spirit, who is in you, whom you have received from God? You are not your own; you were bought at a price. Therefore, honor God with your body.*[117]

God is serious about sexual sin. He is so serious that He not only provides you with His strength, but with a way of escape.

> *No temptation has seized you except what's common to man. And God is faithful; he will not let you be tempted beyond what you can bear. But when you are tempted, he will also provide a way out so that you can stand up under it.*[118]

Here's an example of a way out. One time, while at a restaurant for lunch, Jason felt tempted to look lustfully at a sensually dressed woman. Although he asked God for help in fighting the temptations, during the middle of the lunch Jason could stand it no more and looked at her with lust. When his networking partner asked him to review the situation to see whether there had been a way to avoid it, Jason recalled, "You know, when I first entered the room, a little voice in the back of my head said, 'Sit facing the wall, not the woman.' But the voice was very faint…" In retrospect, Jason realized the Lord had provided him a way of escape after all; he had simply chosen to ignore it.

Need for a Game Plan

Do you have a game plan for dealing with temptations? It's one thing to resolve to build sexual integrity and promise yourself you'll put an end to all sexual fantasies, but it's another to put it into practice.

When a pretty woman in tight clothing walks by, what's your plan for choosing sexual integrity? What will you do to keep from falling into an old, familiar habit of turning her into a sexual fantasy?

Henry not only stared at women with lust in his heart, he took it a step further. He made a regular practice of memorizing images of women to use as a basis for fantasies later. His practice was to give into—not resist—temptation. But as God foretold, the stolen turned sour in his stomach and the burning coals were too much to bear. Henry needed a new game plan. He needed to flee.

A popular book on purity wisely suggests, "bouncing your eyes."[119] This means forming a habit of immediately rejecting sensual inputs by looking away from everything that tempts you to lust. When you see a woman jogger, or an open blouse, or a sexy billboard ad, you bounce your eyes away. I agree that it's vital that you bring to a halt such sensory inputs including bouncing, blinking or blinding your eyes, but both authors would agree that you cannot stop there.

If all you do is distract yourself from temptations without also incorporating all six elements of the PROVEN acronym into your life, you're merely practicing behavior modification. Thus, you remain a self-seeker and self-doer. Under those conditions, you won't receive God's power to overcome. That's because your inner desires and lusts of the world have not changed. As a result, you remain a slave to sexual sin. It also explains why so many never experience true change. Sure, they can go a few weeks or months without looking at porn, but when stress is too great or the right opportunity arises they dive back in.

Looking for a game plan? We're all familiar with the basic 3 Rs of grammar school: *Reading, 'Riting, and 'Rithmetic.*

Well, there also are 3 Rs for addressing temptations:

RECOGNIZE
RUIN
REPLACE

It's not enough to simply look away from suggestive visual images; you must recognize it as sin, ruin the moment, and repent by replacing it with healthy thoughts. Otherwise your mind will seek to replay the short glance and enlarge it through fantasy. In addition, merely bouncing your eyes off of an input (although a good habit) will not lead to lasting change, since it initiates a never-ending contest between temptation and resistance, but does nothing to address sensual desire. Let's consider instead what each of these 3 Rs can do for you.

RECOGNIZE the Sin

Chances are that you aren't fully aware of just how much you let your eyes or mind wander in lust or fantasy. Take stock over the next few days. Notice when you are taking second looks or when you let your mind wander in a sexual manner. You may be very surprised at what you find.

The 3 Rs for Tackling Temptation

Have you ever heard of the "three second rule"? Some say that the definition of an impure thought is staring at a woman for three seconds or more. Three seconds? Baloney! In that amount of time, a man can commit adultery more than three times in his mind!

Measuring sin in seconds takes a shallow view of the God who transcends time. To the Lord, three seconds may as well be three years—or three thousand! Can you imagine talking with God and using this lame excuse, "I limited my lust to three-second spurts"? This reduces God to the mentality of a casual newspaper reader, following glib promises to eliminate sin in three seconds. Actually, allowing yourself three seconds means lust remains an option. Are you really going to pretend that's acceptable? Who do you think you're fooling?

▶ **TIM: Giving up Consolation**

Tim's only safe world had been fantasy, porn and masturbation, so it was especially hard for Tim to agree to stop fantasizing. But Tim had formed a pattern of finding the nearest fast food chain to indulge in a dessert, then using the restroom to masturbate. This was the reason he was both overweight and addicted to masturbation.

Sexual purity was a much taller order for Tim than it is for many men. Tim would make it a few days using his own willpower, but if his dad humiliated him and made him feel worthless, it was often more than Tim could handle. He would take consolation in sexual release.

Once he had joined the group, Tim lied in the beginning, saying that he had not masturbated during the week, but his guilt overwhelmed him. He called the leader and confessed by telephone. The leader told Tim that he loved him and understood his battle. He prayed with Tim and gave him encouragement—without guilt, shame or judgment. Tim gradually realized that the group was really safe and began to confess his setbacks, as well as his victories. As the weeks progressed, Tim had more periods of victory than defeat.

For Tim a 12-week study was too short. Tim begged the leader to let him start again in the next study. Of course, the leader agreed. Tim stopped masturbating weekly. He embraced the belief that God was good and would not discard him. Tim fought hard to use the three Rs; always having a life verse handy reminding him that God didn't condemn him (as his own father had). Tim knew he was forgiven each time and began wanting to please the Lord through purity. God was meeting with Tim. He felt that God did love him after all. Tim was finally willing to do whatever it takes—God's way this time.

RUIN the Moment

After you've trained yourself to notice it—as soon as you have an impure thought—you're ready for the next step: You must *ruin* the thought.

Ruin means just that—"ruin the moment." This involves a decision to refuse to indulge the thought even for a moment—whether it's new or a replay of a previous thought. This means ruining *every* impure thought. This is part of the goal and plan of Scripture that commands us to, "demolish arguments and every pretension that sets itself up against the knowledge of God, and we take captive every thought to make it obedient to Christ."[120]

How do you do that? Reject every single thought or temptation. Reject them the moment they occur. Don't give them an inch or a home. Keep at it no matter how often you find yourself facing impure thoughts.

It's a difficult transition; moving from enjoying fleeting sexual thoughts to deliberately rejecting them. It may mean that at first you actually say to your own thought: "I take no pleasure from you."

▶ **JOEL: Learning to Ruin the Moment**

Because I had spent 20 years sexualizing everything, the temptations to lust kept knocking at my door every moment of every day. Each morning I had to make a new commitment to purity. For the first few weeks, it seemed as if I were confessing sexual thoughts every minute of my subway commute, but I was determined. So I developed a game plan for my commute. I brought a Bible study with me to read while seated and look only at the ground while walking, since each time I had looked above a woman's ankles, I was tempted to think about her in a sexual way.

I was determined to recognize each and every impure thought. For instance, if a woman sat in the seat next to me, and if I glanced at her and noticed her bust, I would close my eyes or look away to ruin the moment immediately. I would acknowledge and confess the thought as sinful and ask God for forgiveness. I would then immediately replace the thought by reading a Bible verse.

It was not easy. It felt like I was in a foxhole during a war. I might easily confess ten times to lustful thoughts during my 45 minute commute to work. Each time I would keep repeating, "not an option, not an option," in order to ruin the moment. I couldn't let the thought linger or it would fuel my old nature where I ultimately would replay the thought while masturbating. But now, it was no longer an option. Yet, at times, the image of a woman kept appearing in my mind, so I would repeat to myself: "I refuse to take pleasure." I did this each time a tempting thought tried entering my mind. It often took a few times of repeating this for the image to fade away. At times, that was not even enough and I had to rapidly blink my eyes to erase the image. I would also replace the thought with something pure, such as the wonderful wife God had provided or a verse of Scripture spelling out one of the promises of God.

In the early days, I would have an internal discussion that went something like this: "Lust is a sin. God hates sin. Therefore, I hate to lust." Sometimes I had to repeat it three times to drown out the small voice that murmured in the back of my head, "What's the big deal? No one is hurt."

But I trusted God and wanted to retrain my backward thinking. Therefore, I reminded myself all day every day that lust, pornography, and masturbation were unwelcome in my life.

After a few weeks, I knew that I had to stop watching television because I lusted after the actresses. Even watching football was not safe due to the commercials. I had such a resolve for holiness that I eventually gave up all movies and TV for an entire year.

Initially, my wife was upset because that meant we couldn't watch TV together. At first, we just sat on the couch, looking at each other and wondering what we would do to replace our TV time. But when we began playing board games together, we started to get to know each other for the first time. We began talking and sharing. To our surprise, giving up TV was the best thing that had happened to us.

I was no longer content to wait until the end of the day or week to recount and confess the sexual sinful thoughts and repent. I repented on the spot, even as I pushed a sexual thought from my mind. This was one of the keys that kept me from returning to the lifelong habit of masturbating each day. I realized that if I ruined every sexual thought in my mind, it would be impossible to masturbate again.

REPLACE the Thought

It's not enough to try to block sexual thoughts. In those few seconds before you reject the sexual thoughts and images that come into your mind, you have sinned. Remember, God doesn't go by the three second rule. Eliminating the thoughts after you have had them is not enough to build sexual integrity or stamp you PROVEN. Each time you sin, you must repent so God can forgive you and you can be reconciled with Him.

Consider this passage:

> *When an unclean spirit goes out of a man, he goes through dry places, seeking rest, and finds none. Then he says, "I will return to my house from which I came." And when he comes, he finds it empty, swept, and put in order. Then he goes and takes with him seven other spirits more wicked than himself, and they enter and dwell there; and the last state of that man is worse than the first. So shall it also be with this wicked generation.*[121]

It's not enough to empty your house (heart) of impurity one time. Otherwise, you may as well place a huge "vacancy" advertisement on the front door, inviting all comers to enter. You already know that the Lord doesn't force you to meet with Him or to remain holy, but softly calls out to you for fellowship. The world, on the other hand, pushes and shoves to get ahead, seeking to drag others down with it.

If the devil cannot shame you into avoiding confessing your sins and repenting in the first place, he'll try to convince you that you need only divert your eyes away after you have sinned. Don't forget that the Lord says, *"If we confess our sins,* he is faithful and just and will forgive us our sins and purify us from all unrighteousness."[122]

It doesn't say if you stop sinning, He forgives. Rather, you must confess and repent. That means you must confess every sin and *turn* from it. The best way to do that is confess it as sin the moment it occurs and then repent and replace the thought.

Satan is a master at deception. He can even try to make you think that all you need to do is sign-up for a 12-week purity program and that'll be good enough; you can keep running the rest of your life as before without true change or repentance. The devil's goal is to make your final condition even worse. Don't you see?

You must not just *recognize* the thoughts, but *ruin* and *replace* them. Replacement is the heart of repentance. Repentance begins by confessing the thought as sinful, then asking God for forgiveness. Reconciliation with God is maintained by changing your conduct and attitude. It is about being constantly on guard and then ruining and replacing any intruding thoughts.

Don't just sweep clean your mind. Replace the sinful thoughts with Godly thoughts. The Bible says, "Set your mind on things above, not on earthly things. For you died, and your life is now hidden with Christ."[123] The Bible also tells you what you should *replace* such thoughts with: "... whatever is true, whatever is noble, whatever is right, whatever is pure, whatever is lovely, whatever is admirable—if anything is excellent or praiseworthy—think about such things."[124]

▶ STAN: Ruining and Replacing

At every corner on campus, there was a pretty woman. Stan needed to take captive every thought and conform it to Christ. The three Rs were helpful to Stan. At first, it was amazing to realize just how much he was looking with lust at women. Dozens of times a day he caught himself daydreaming about sex or taking second looks. Stan was doing more than just looking—he was memorizing women's bodies, comparing or rating them in his mind. Sometimes his friends would even joke about what score to give a girl that walked by or would nudge him to take notice of someone.

Stan made a decision to stop allowing these thoughts to fill his mind. He began to practice "ruining and replacing." Each time he began thinking sexual thoughts about a woman, he would confess it as sin. During battles, he would constantly say to himself, "ruin and replace." Even as the thought tried to creep back in, Stan would not take any pleasure from it. Stan also began taking the Proven Men weekly memory verses with him to aid him in the battle and to replace the daydreaming.

Stan also told his friends that he didn't want to listen to sexual jokes or play the rating game anymore. He was even brave enough to tell them that he was interested in purity and mentioned that he was attending a sexual integrity group. He told them he had given up pornography and was attending Proven Men meetings. He suggested that they check out the Proven Men website.

Making it Work

Each time you have a lustful thought, recognize it quickly and stop it in its tracks. Acknowledge it as selfish and wrong by repenting and confessing it to God as sin. If you do this, you won't end up looking at pornography or masturbating. You simply cannot engage in sexual sin when you cut to shreds every tempting thought.

Each time you stumble, tell the Lord of your sorrow for turning away from Him, expressing to God your desire to be forgiven. Turn back to God right away by accepting His forgiveness and restoration. Finally, put a pure thought in your mind, such as a Bible verse or spiritual song.

Temptation to lust is not an easy battle to win. It keeps attacking and attracting you many times a day. In fact, it's only natural to expect that your subconscious mind will suggest that you think about things you used to think about in the past. Be patient. It can take weeks to retrain your mind to dwell on holy and pure thoughts. Expect it to take a lot of effort. It will. But all of the men who have been stamped PROVEN can attest to the fact that it is possible. If they can do it, so can you. So be on guard.

As you learn to consistently ruin lustful thoughts and replace them with passion for God, you'll renew your mind. You won't forever be a slave to your old pattern of thinking, which was fixated on satisfying your selfish cravings. Satan will eventually tire of suggesting lustful thoughts if you constantly choose to immediately replace them with thoughts pleasing to God. Of course, the devil will return to tempt you again when you are tired, stressed, or acting in your own strength. So, expect a lifetime battle.

Consistency is the key. You must Recognize, Ruin and Replace every impure thought—even if it means repenting every 30 seconds! Don't retreat an inch!

In time, this process will become second nature. Don't give up the fight! Keep asking God for His power over lust and rely on it. Then keep Resting daily in the Lord in all areas of your life. That's the hallmark of a Proven Man.

Don't Be an Independent Torch Bearer

There's a hidden problem with giving you a list of 3 Rs to use in the battle against temptation. You may become focused too heavily upon a goal of getting rid of the behavior rather than righting your relationship with the Lord. Allow me to explain. You were created to be a servant of the Lord. Yet your human nature wants to be independent. You want to be in control and run the show.

As a result, Christian men tend to get consumed with *doing for* God rather than *being with* Him. In other words, you'll be tempted to take the 3 Rs as your duty to achieve sexual integrity, forgetting that the ultimate goal isn't to simply reduce the sin, but to link your heart with the Lord so that your desires become His desires. This is what truly results in purity.

Consider an analogy.

Men are a lot like light bulbs. They tend to go through life thinking that they (the light bulbs) are the source of power and light and have no need for outside power (God). In reality, when you go your own way apart from God, you actually are unscrewing the light bulb from the socket. The longer you stay unplugged, the easier a time you have deceiving yourself that you're still producing light. The Bible talks about this type of light bulb,

> *Who among you fears the Lord and obeys the word of his servant? Let the one who walks in the dark, who has no light, trust in the name of the Lord and rely on their God. But now, all you who light fires and provide yourselves with flaming torches, go, walk in the light of your fires and of the torches you have set ablaze. This is what you shall receive from my hand: You will lie down in torment.*[125]

God warns that those who walk in the darkness (apart from God), who light their own fires (self-effort) and follow their own ways will not experience God's healing, but instead remain in torment. The path of the independent firelighter is heading straight for the acts of the sinful nature.

Firelighters include those who carry the scars of the past, vowing never to be hurt again. They live a life of independence from anyone or anything, including God. However, your deepest scars can only be healed through a soothing life of dependency upon God. You're deceived and following the wrong path if you're seeking to be healed (or protected from further harm) by yourself.

God is calling you to dip your torch into His cool stream of living water and with it extinguishing your flames of retribution, anger, a closed heart, independence and bitterness. These are just some of the fruits of walking in your own strength. Of course, sexual impurity is another one of these poisonous fruits of self-effort or independence. God, however, wants to light the path for you, taking you into a green pasture where you will enjoy the fruit of the Spirit.

Chapter 11

The Two Keys to Victory

When a man is nearly drowning in his struggle with an addictive behavior, it takes more than knowledge of the Proven Path to break free. It requires a resolve and determination for absolute purity and sexual integrity. You've probably made commitments for purity in the past. But it didn't last. Something was still missing.

Wouldn't you like to know what other men are saying are the keys to their lasting victory? Most men who have broken free from sexual addiction share two keys to victory.

First, they took on a new mindset that sexual sins, such as pornography and fantasy, are *not an option*. That's because when you say you'll try harder to give up a selfish practice, it actually leaves room for you to give in to that sin if things get too hard. It must not be an option, period—no matter how hard it gets.

Second, they resolved to do *whatever it took* to fulfill their new primary commitment. This time, they decided to do it God's way. They put down the shovel of self-effort and held nothing back from the Lord.

Not an Option

You can only serve one master.[126] Either you are with Christ or on the side of the devil in the battle between good and evil. Satan will lead you to a path of surrendering your position in God's kingdom by offering you affairs, sexual love, and fantasy. Don't be deceived. You cannot warm your hands at the enemy's fire and not get burned, captured, and destroyed. Actually, the sexual weapon being used today is an effective age-old trick.

When Israel was preparing to take over the Promised Land, the kings currently holding the position were frightened.[127] They knew that they couldn't fight against the God who parted the Red Sea forty years prior[128] and who just parted the Jordan River as they were currently advancing.[129]

The King of Moab knew he needed help. His first attempt was bribing Balaam to cast a curse on Israel.[130] Four times, however, the Lord prevented Balaam from being able to curse Israel.[131] Because God was too strong, Balaam told Moab that he first needed to lure the people away from the Lord. He proposed using sex as the bait.[132] Moab agreed. He sent the nation's most seductive women to the frontlines hoping to lure the men of Israel away from serving their God through salivating over selfish sexual secret sauces. It nearly worked too, with many Israelites agreeing to worship idols in exchange for sexual favors from the Moabite women.[133]

The fall was so rapid and far reaching that one man brazenly brought a Moabite woman directly back into God's camp in front of Moses' own eyes.[134] The Moabite enemy knew that a holy God would have to depart from the household of sin. They need not fight God directly if His children embrace sin and push God aside. However, God brought a plague upon the Israelites to wake them up. It ended only as Proven Men forsook sexual sin and removed those who would not repent. Once the nation turned back to God, the Lord moved mightily and supplied all their true needs, as well as granting them victory over Moab and his nation.[135]

Did you ever wonder why the divorce rate is so high, even among Christians? In today's culture, divorce is an option. Some openly admit that their marriage motto is: "I'll stay married as long as I get something out of it." Most conceal the truth about this selfish belief about marriage and their unwillingness to put their mate first. To them, divorce remains an option, even if that option is buried deep within their heart. They enter marriage with a bailout clause if it costs them too much.

The same applies to Christians giving in to sexual sin. Some still secretly consider limited viewing of pornography, taking second looks at women, and hiding in fantasy as "options" in their lives. Whenever sin is an option, however, it's just a matter of time or an event before it's acted upon. Besides, when sin remains an option, your heart has already sinned. It's trusting in the future prospect of a worldly fix, not the power of God. Such a man has failed to make a covenant with his eyes not to look with lust upon women[136] nor relied upon the Lord to give him the strength to carry it out.

It's time for you to stop playing games with sexual sin. Will you make this covenant with yourself before God that your preferred sexual sinful practices are *no longer an option*? You must fill in the specific sexual sin that has ensnared you, whether it's pornography, masturbation or fantasy. In other words, you must say: *Pornography is no longer an option in my life.* Go ahead and make that commitment now. Fill in whatever sin that plagues you.

If you don't do this, you'll fail. Refusing to make it "no longer an option" is one of the single most common reasons why a man doesn't break free from sexual sin.

Most men are too afraid to make the determination that pornography or sexual fantasy is "no longer an option" because they think they need that escape route. But, it's time for you to draw a line and tell Satan he no longer has control over you through sexual sin. Please, dear brother, right now make this irrevocable decision that pornography and sexual fantasy are no longer an option.

Doing Whatever It Takes

When I committed to the truth that sexual fantasies and masturbation were no longer options, I was scared to death. How could I just stop a habit of 20 years? It didn't matter what the cost; I vowed I would never masturbate again, period. Yet, I knew that I could not win on my own. I knew that the only way to follow through on that commitment was to add the second part of the equation: To be willing to do whatever it took; God's way this time.

It's not enough to make an oath that your sexual sin is no longer an option. You must become *a doer* of God's Word.[137] Thus, the second key to lasting victory is being *willing to do whatever it takes* to stop allowing sexual sin to be an option. Nothing can be off limits.

For instance, if you keep lusting while driving past a certain place on the way home from work, change your route home. If you keep lusting after your secretary, then change jobs. If you keep lusting at the gym or a certain magazine rack, stop going to that place. If you look for ways to get around your Internet filter, stop using the computer. For a season be willing to stop going to the mall, Starbucks or any other place where you are commonly tempted. Are you getting the picture? You must be willing to eliminate everything that makes you more vulnerable to going astray.

Consider the command the Lord gave to Israel after defeating Moab. God told Israel that as it drove out the nations from the Promised Land that they must totally destroy them.[138] This point was so important that thirteen chapters later the Bible repeats it and explains why. The Israelites were told to destroy everything that breathes, "Otherwise they will teach you to follow all the detestable things they do in worshipping their gods, and you will sin against the Lord your God."[139]

Notice that God allowed Israel to take over the Promised Land in stages, so the land would not be barren. Israel started strong. As it moved through the land, it completely destroyed the inhabitants of the cities in each territory. After Joshua had died, there was still land that needed to be taken. But the Israelites didn't obey God. Instead, "when Israel became strong, they pressed the Canaanites into forced labor but never drove them out completely."[140]

Although it may have seemed like a good idea to gain slaves, it was disobedient. They forgot the reason why God told them to drive the nations out—that they would pick up bad habits from the inhabitants and end up turning away from God to sin. The Lord was angry at their disobedience and told the nation that, since it had refused to drive them all out, the Lord would allow the other nations to remain in the land, where they would be constant thorns in their sides and their false gods would be a snare.[141] And that's exactly what happened. Israel ended up chasing idols of the other nations, and still today there are other nations occupying their country.

The same is true for you. You cannot play games with lust. You must totally destroy this idol in your life. You must rid your house and environment of all things that ensnare. Right now, think about whether you are allowing the idols of the world to be close to home. For instance, when you allow pornography to be at your fingertips, you'll eventually turn to it. It may mean not having Internet in your house or on your cell telephone. Similarly, if you keep going to places where you are tempted to lust, you will eventually lust. Therefore, places like the gym or a magazine rack need to be off limits.

Let's return to the main point. Are you willing to do *whatever it takes* to experience God's healing and stay within His borders? Are you also willing to remove all idols from your life? You know yourself, what idols remain in your environment that are easily accessed? It's time to uproot them all!

It may be easy for you to say "yes," but knowing what to do and then carrying it out is another matter entirely. A fine sounding cliché won't transform you. The underlying Proven Path needs to be fully embraced. It means knowing and acting upon a desire to be "willing to do whatever it takes."

You aren't willing to do whatever it takes if some part of the sexual impurity process still remains *an option*, whether it's pre-marital sex, affairs, pornography, masturbation, chat room flings, or lustful thoughts. Real freedom in life is thwarted if you retain an active fantasy life. That's where the sin begins.

If you're married, don't fool yourself into thinking that an affair "just happens." As discussed earlier, there's a clear process. You first start getting complacent. You entertain lustful thoughts and even fantasize about having sex with someone. It's just a matter of time before you start acting on your fantasies.

To avoid having an affair, you must also make a permanent decision that masturbation, pornography, affairs, and the like are not options. Otherwise, when the temptations arise, you will not be ready to say no. That's also why a game plan is so important. You make a plan on how to say no to temptations and to flee, not flirt with them.

For single men, pornography or its accompanying masturbation doesn't just happen. You don't need to be a slave to it. Again, there's a clear progression. You first allow your mind to dwell on something sexual. You fuel the hormones that pump through your body; all the second looks you take or fantasies you allow start to build up inside of you. Then, when you are bored, lonely, or stressed, or your guard is down or weakened, you give in.

If you put into practice your commitment that these sins are not an option and combine that with a daily practice of relying on the 3 Rs (recognize, ruin and replace), you won't look at porn and masturbate.

The reason why I have not masturbated in over 15 years is not because I am married. I was masturbating almost daily for seven years into my marriage. It was that I took on an attitude that it's *no longer an option* period, then cut to shreds every lustful thought. I refused to take any pleasure from them. I didn't wait 3 or 30 seconds to ruin the moment. I did it the instant I recognized the impure thought. (My freedom from masturbation or pornography, however, will last only as long as I continue this process as part of daily living out the elements of a Proven life.)

The same victory is true for Stan. He's single and has a girlfriend, but stopped entertaining lustful thoughts. He stopped looking at pornography and eyeing other women. Killing those inputs killed the need to masturbate. Of course, he also had to make a firm commitment and then do business with setting boundaries with being with Missy to avoid premarital sex.

Commit right now that you'll no longer have any escape clauses. Commit that pornography, masturbation, sex outside of marriage, and fantasies are no longer options. Be willing to do whatever it takes to fulfill your vows. Hold nothing back, including certain music, TV shows, or the gym, if they cause you to stumble. You know yourself and what you have been holding onto. Confess them and then turn from them.

But don't forget that when you sweep your house clean, there is a void that will be filled. That's why you must "replace" your lustful thoughts with things of the Spirit. That's why you must include all six elements of the Proven Path into your daily life.

▶ JOEL: Filling an Empty Room

I had not really wanted to be well for 20 years. I merely wanted the struggle to go away. I hated the guilt and shame, but secretly loved the pleasurable parts of fantasy and masturbation. Deep inside I knew that I didn't want to give God control of the part of my life that would keep fantasy as an escape option. I felt I needed that crutch.

When I finally made masturbation and my connected fantasy world no longer an option, I was scared because that was my treasured secret escape. Not wanting to ever return back to that double-agent life, I became desperate for Christ to fill the empty room and to give me strength. I trusted the Lord by giving Him my whole heart, this time every square inch. I gave God access to and control over my thought life. I truly wanted to get well. I took on Galatians 2:20 as my life verse to combat self-pride; I died to self and agreed to live in and through the Lord. I was done trusting in my abilities. I was putting God in charge of all areas of my life.

It would be the hardest battle of my life, but it was also the sweetest one. Part of doing whatever it takes was relying daily upon the Lord for strength. From a proud self-doer, I became a needy, dependent servant of Christ. I began experiencing true and daily intimacy with the Lord for the first time. I also no longer had secrets to keep. I felt free. As a result, my relationship with my wife began to flourish. It was even better in all areas than when we first married!

What Is Your Option?

Some men assume that pornography is still an option. If they are confronted, they only make game of stopping. They have preset limits as to what they are willing to do. They may install an Internet filter, for instance, but then plan ways to find pornography online, in times of need. Proof that it remains an option may be found in a refusal to make even some fairly minor changes in these men's routines or lives. They wouldn't consider such simple solutions as changing routes home, throwing away hidden pictures, disconnecting Cable TV, or stop hanging out at magazine racks or Internet hot spots.

For most, the price that's just too costly is confessing to another man or maintaining regular accountability. Inside their hearts is the notion, "I'll do anything but tell another man." This is a real issue for so many men. Both Joel and Tim had sworn oaths to themselves that they would never tell another living soul that they masturbated or looked at pornography. They simply built into their lives the option that they still could do those things.

It may be that you are *unwilling to stop* watching TV, giving up secular music for Christian artists, canceling a gym membership, dropping magazine subscriptions, disconnecting Internet from your cell phone, discarding mementoes of past relationships, ending flirting, eliminating the sharing of personal details with female co-workers, or throwing out everything used as a prelude to or during the activity of sin. The man that keeps these in place regards pornography and masturbation as options.

Are you holding onto any of these things just in case they're needed? If so, you can expect to fail again and again. The only way out is making an irrevocable decision that no matter what it costs you won't ever turn to pornography or sexual fantasy. Then follow through with replacement.

▶ STAN: Building God into His Life

There were times in Stan's life where he used to suffer such a caustic reaction in his body when tempted to seek out Internet pornography, that his stomach hurt. In those instances of intense attack, he eventually and always gave in. Although there was definitely spiritual warfare going on, the root issue was that pornography remained an option for him. Freedom from pornography arrived only when he made an irrevocable commitment that it's no longer an option. He finally realized that because pornography was an option, the intense desire raged on. It was only when his mind and body began accepting that never again would pornography be allowed, that they stopped begging for it. Of course, it was hard. He still had some stomach pain at first, but Stan would put his game plan in place, such as go jogging and flee the temptation. Stan also gave up Internet access on his cell telephone.

What about Missy? At first, Stan didn't want to make a commitment that heavy petting with his girlfriend was not an option. He justified it in many ways, such as they were going to get married anyway, and that what they were doing was not really pre-marital sex, and that no one was getting hurt. But it was affecting their relationship. They both felt the weight of guilt. Finally, Stan took a stand for sexual integrity in this area. Premarital sex would not remain an option.

The evidence that Stan truly made this commitment was evident by what he did. He set limits on their dates, including never being alone with Missy. That's right, never alone with his fiancée! This was one of the hardest battles of his life. It was even harder for Stan than giving up pornography.

Stan wanted to be with Missy all the time, but the "never alone" rule was constricting. It was hard to always be in a group or in a public place. Yet Stan embraced that it was not about following a man-made rule, but that the Lord truly had something better for them. What they did prior to marriage did matter and affect their future marriage.

Stan also began deepening his reliance on, and relationship with, the Lord. In addition to his own "quiet time" with the Lord, on every date they would read the Bible together. He was actually building God into his life and future marriage, not just doing what Christians think they are supposed to do.

Are Lustful Thoughts an Option?

Sexual sins don't just happen; they begin with lust in the heart. As your mind dwells upon sensual imagery, actions become justified and condoned. Eventually, sin moves from the mind to the body. The greater you entertain fantasy and other forms of sensual inputs, the more you increase your struggle to remain physically pure. It's little wonder some men have "high" sex drives. They open their minds up to tremendous volumes of sensual inputs. Please don't misunderstand. God did create each of us sexual and unique, but as we allow our minds to wander we heighten even more the God-given desires. The point is that all men need to curtail their inputs and conform their thoughts to the pattern of Christ.

In truth, most men permit themselves occasional lustful thoughts and second looks. It remains more than an option—they subconsciously build it into their daily life. They are unaware that one of the ways Satan binds men is convincing them to retain fantasies as an option.

I know a man named Randy who was satisfied once he seemed able to rid his life of pornography. Unfortunately, he didn't fully address his inner lust and fantasies. Actually, he kept them as his escape clause. Little did Randy realize just how much it thwarted true victory. His marriage was always a bumpy ride. That's because parts of his heart and mind were still given over to the enemy. Randy fell for the same trap as the legalistic Pharisees who wanted to know which law was most important, with his own backward thinking: "If I can just stop looking at pornography, I will be holy."

It doesn't work that way. You must desire to be holy because God is holy. It isn't enough to rid yourself of the one sin you dislike.

It's time for you to begin to recognize just how many sexual fantasies you're allowing in your life. Don't be deceived; a man reaps what he sows. If your heart is chasing after things off limits, you'll venture out of bounds. Besides, aren't you really telling God you aren't content with the life He gave you?

▶ TIM: Giving Up His Life

After going through the Proven Men purity study twice, Tim stopped looking at porn or daily masturbating (although still stumbling on a few occasions). Even though Tim was head and shoulders above where he began, he was not experiencing the fullness of intimacy with his wife, both emotionally and sexually. He and his wife started attending marriage counseling, but couldn't put their finger on the problem. Finally, his Proven Men small group leader suggested that there was something Tim was still holding back in his relationship, the same reason why he occasionally returned to masturbation. The leader asked Tim to make an irrevocable decision that *masturbation was no longer an option,* such that he would give up anything that contributed to his fall. That meant nothing could be off limits, even refusing to travel for his job. This jolted Tim. Up until then, Tim thought that he had given up masturbation. Now he realized that he had been unwilling to risk everything to remain pure. He knew he had never really committed in his heart that it was never an option.

That day Tim fell before God and put his entire life and his job on the altar. No matter what the cost, masturbation was no longer an option, period. Almost immediately, Tim's intimacy with his wife began to flourish. Something inside him just clicked when he made this covenant. It was now just he and his wife, period. Thus, if he had a fight with his wife, he couldn't slip away into fantasy. He had to deal with her and real life without any escapes. This ushered in change and dependency on the Lord!

Tim also began taking risks opening up to his wife in new and intimate ways. It was remarkable how his wife was responding. She commented that it was like they were having the honeymoon they never had. His wife was so excited about the change that she used the *Proven Men* study as her next Bible study. She wanted to be stamped a *Proven Woman!* That was the restart of the relationship they never had, but always wanted! This is the story of a man who once thought the best option was suicide!

Tim was finally finished running from reality. He was done pretending all was well. He trusted that he didn't need to escape into fantasy. He believed that the life God had for him would be sufficient. He trusted that he could be vulnerable and open with his wife, despite the pain that goes along with real relationships.

Rocking the Boat

Are you ready to really rock the boat? Are you willing to fully embrace all of God's ways, no matter what the cost? Are you willing to throw overboard all your sexual fantasies?

Consider this: God tells you to take captive *every* thought—not just sexual fantasies—and make it obedient to Christ.[142]

It's time to get radical with sin. Go ahead. Throw overboard *all* fantasies. We are talking about fantasies where you're acting as a hero saving the life of the president, winning the lottery, and other selfish ways you dream of having an easy life. It also encompasses those darker images where you replay in your mind images of taking revenge against a boss or getting even with someone who hurt you.

Of course, not every daydream is a sin, but all too often we escape into selfish fantasies that do hinder our real relationships. If you take the time to examine many of your non-sexual fantasies and daydreaming, you'll find that some, if not most, are just as much pride-based selfish desires as your sexual fantasies. This is the stuff that blocks you from really trusting God.

Think about it. Isn't the secret place in your mind where you pretend to be more handsome and witty, and have other features, characteristics and traits that are more wonderful than in real life? Aren't these fantasies your Christmas "wish list" for all the things you wished you had and for "acting out" the person you wished you could be?

Living in reality is the path to a new pure thought life. Therefore, stop being content to merely rid sexual fantasies from your life; be holy across the board as your Heavenly Father is holy. My dear brothers, whenever you seek to live inside a make-believe world, you're telling God, in effect, that He made a mistake in your life, that He is not good, that He cannot provide for you and, worse, that you can do a better job with the shovel.

If you find that you aren't grateful and content in your life, you may need to consider the effects of your dreaming of living a life that does not and could never really exist. Hiding in fantasy pushes aside the only One who can meet your true needs by refusing to allow Him to direct your real life. It's time to stop pretending. It's time to stop washing just the outside of your cup.

Put Sin on the Altar

Are you ready to do business with sin and embrace sexual integrity? Put all of your secret sexual outlets on the altar and kill them. That's right. Destroy everything that sets itself up between you and God. Give it to the Lord. A good test of your conviction, faith, and action is making this irrevocable commitment in prayer:

> Lord, I am willing to do whatever it takes. My sins (list them) are no longer an option. I yield my life, my mind, my body, my heart, and my soul completely to you. This time I commit all areas. I hold nothing back. I give up my rights and expectations. I lay down the shovel of self-effort. I will seek your will and obey your desires. I exchange my life for yours, now and forever. I commit to living out a Proven life, applying each element daily into my life through your grace and by your power.
>
> Dated: _____   Signed: _____

Did you make this Prayer? If so, congratulations! You now are stamped a Proven Man. (Go ahead and date and sign the commitment.)

Because God is now the one in charge, you will live victoriously.

Will the battles be easy, now that returning to these things are no longer options? Of course it won't. In the short run, it will seem even harder to enjoy the victory God already won for you because you no longer will turn to the temporary pain numbing medication of fantasy or sexual exploits. You'll taste the pain of battle as all soldiers of Christ do. But, what's the alternative? The war is already lost if an aspect of sinning remains an option. So, fight hard, but do so in God's strength!

Now that sexual sins are not options, you must refuse to take any pleasure from them, not even for a moment. You set a bouncer at the door and take captive every thought. Be sure to include another of your new mottos, *ruin and replace*. When prior sexual images or unclean thoughts enter your mind, make it a practice to actually say in your mind: "I take no pleasure from you." Cut off the thought mid-stream. Don't let it finish. Then confess the thought as sinful and ask for forgiveness. Keep asking God for His power, and rely on it. You must follow this practice every single time you lust, even if it's every 30 seconds! Then immediately replace the thought with something true, right or noble.

In times when the battle is fierce, retain your conviction that giving in is not an option. When tempting thoughts pressed upon Joel's mind, he kept repeating to himself, "not an option, not an option, not an option" and then relied on God's strength to purpose to replace the thought with a Bible verse or something praiseworthy.

Cling all the more to the Lord and rely upon His power. And, when you stumble, or shall we call it for what it really is—when you take back control of your life and *sin*—you race back to the Lord. Remember, a setback does *not* mean that you are no longer a Proven Man. You're now and forever a Proven Man, so embrace it.

The measure of a Proven Man is not how many times he takes a hit in battle, but by how quickly and strongly he purposes to daily living out each element of a Proven life together with the Lord. Therefore, keep **p**assionately praising God, **r**epenting over each and every sin, **o**pening up your heart, soul and mind to the perfecting fire of God, walking in God's **v**ictory, not your own strength, renewing your **e**ternal perspective through reading the Bible, and staying **n**etworking with and encouraging one another.

Chapter 12

Finishing the Race

For nearly 20 years, I was sickened by my daily turning to masturbation. I hated the guilt and shame. Therefore, I pleaded almost daily with God to take away the temptations. I couldn't understand why God didn't answer these prayers. After all, surely God wanted me free from sexual bondage.

Despite my so-called good intentions, I had misunderstood. God didn't merely want me ending a sinful practice that I felt was disgusting. God wanted an intimate relationship with me.

Are you like me? Have you spent endless hours begging God to take away the sexual temptations? That's not God's way. If God had just taken away the temptations, I would have remained proud and even boasted about how I had overcome sexual sin on my own. God loved me too much to take away the temptations and leave me as a puffed up sinner.

Every now and then, you do hear the occasional story where God simply took away the desire of a man to look at pornography and he was instantly freed. That's great, but the Lord must have had a different reason in that person's life. For me, and the remaining

99.99 percent of us, God chooses to heal from sexual sin slowly on purpose.

Consider Apostle Paul. After Jesus personally appeared to him, Paul was given a divine mission. It is clear Paul was willing to do whatever it took to accomplish that mission. He was flogged five times, beaten with rods three times, stoned once, shipwrecked (spending a full day in the ocean), and was left cold and naked without sleep or food.[143] Paul was a Proven Man. Yet, he had one thing he couldn't overcome.

Paul had a thorn in his flesh. We don't really know what it was, whether it was a physical illness or a struggle with a sin common to man. That doesn't matter. But what does matter is Paul's example. Listen to him describe the situation.

> *To keep me from becoming conceited because of these surpassingly great revelations, there was given me a thorn in my flesh, a messenger of Satan, to torment me. Three times I pleaded with the Lord to take it away from me. But he said to me, "My grace is sufficient for you, for my power is made perfect in weakness." Therefore I will boast all the more gladly about my weaknesses, so that Christ's power may rest on me. That's why, for Christ's sake, I delight in weaknesses, in insults, in hardships, in persecutions, in difficulties. For when I am weak, then I am strong.[144]*

Paul had repeatedly asked the Lord to take away the thorn, but God had chosen not to. Paul didn't shrink, but quickly accepted that it was his cross to carry. He was willing to daily rely on God's strength and grace. He also was glad that the Lord put this one thing in his life that he couldn't overcome on his own to keep him from being conceited or puffed up, as pride is what always moves us away from the Lord. Remember, the same "conceit" or pride Paul knew would keep him apart from God is the same root that feeds sexual sin. Be glad the Lord doesn't just take away your painful thorn.

Slow on Purpose

Have you accepted that God's timing is perfect? This applies to all areas of your life—getting married, finding a job, healing old wounds, or becoming free from certain sins. God has a purpose behind everything. Sexual healing is often slow because the Lord is taking you at a pace you can handle. Just as you would not send a child down a steep hill the first time they learned to ride a bike, so God won't bring you through the healing process at a faster pace than you can learn, appreciate, and accept. God wants to provide you with lasting healing, not merely a Band-Aid.

Accept that the process of healing goes on for a lifetime. That's why we even call our 12-week *Study* just the fundamentals, and not the finish line to dealing with lust.

Please don't be discouraged that it's a lifelong process; there still will be moments of significant strides along the way. Be glad that you are told that it will be a long and difficult process. It's time to put on an *eternal perspective* and the mind of Christ and to fight against the tactics of Satan.

The devil's tricks include trying to fill your mind with thoughts of self-effort. For others, he tries to make you think you need to earn God's love or approval. Thus, when you have a setback, you hide from God, worried that you didn't earn His love.

For each of us, when our guard is down, Satan seeks to turn our thoughts inward and focused upon our circumstances and rights. Expect that the devil will flood your mind with tempting thoughts to chase after the momentary pleasures of the world, while trying to shield you from the true nature and cost of such things. Satan also deceptively makes the little sins in life (such as gossip or anger) seem too insignificant to bother with, because he knows that if you give him a foothold in "little" areas, he can gain more control in your life.

Don't fall for Satan's lies as he tries telling you that the pace is going too slow and that you need to pick up the shovel of self-effort. Guard against the temptation to take back control when you think the process is going too slow. That's a product of pride.

Similarly, stop comparing yourself to others. God has a plan and pace designed just for you. Yes, be encouraged by the testimonies of others, but don't allow judging thoughts to take hold. That means not judging another man whose pace is slower than yours. It also means not beating yourself up or quitting if your pace is the slower one.

Did you notice that for Joel, one time through a 12-week purity *Study* was all that was needed to stop masturbating, but for Tim, it took three times through the *Study,* or a year and one-half? If Tim got stuck comparing his life to Joel's, he would have felt defeated and given up. So stop comparing and keep your eyes on the Lord.

Be encouraged. Remember, although sexual integrity is a lifelong process, you'll experience great victories along the way. Of course, you'll still have struggles and occasional setbacks, but you can walk in victory as you continually repent of any sin and daily turn to and rely upon God. Keep the E *(Eternal in Perspective)* in PROVEN always before you. In other words, don't be consumed with how long it takes to see "the results." Concentrate on today.[145] Besides, the real result is an intimate relationship—which is a growing experience.

In addition, don't be discouraged if you don't feel like a spiritual giant in the early stages. At four weeks into fighting for sexual integrity, I was still staring at the ground most of the time because I still tended to lust after women I would see during my commute. Yet, I was not consumed with counting the number of days in which I acted (or failed to act) in freedom because I was too busy clinging to and seeking the Lord in desperation and dependency. I finally appreciated that I simply couldn't ever overcome on my own.

Be mindful that God won't act outside your will. He only works in a willing heart, one that's not proud or stubborn. He will wait until you are ready. So cooperate with Him.

Just as sanctification or spiritual maturity is a lifelong process, so is building sexual integrity. Be excited about the process, because it's a process of God; one with a divine purpose of preparing you for deep intimacy with Him and for you to conform your desires and life to the perfect will of the Father.

Today, be committed to loving God and hating evil. Tomorrow will take care of itself, if you trust God that is! Your job is to participate with God. Don't take back control or think you can do it on your own. Rather, truly desire to be transformed. If you secretly want to enjoy the sensual pleasures of pornography or lust, God's transformation process will be thwarted. Remember, God's goal is for you to live out a Proven life, beginning with being passionate for him.

Climbing a Moving Ladder

You can never let up in striving for sexual integrity because life is like climbing a moving ladder that is always descending. If you simply hang on, you'll be pulled down. It takes great effort to go against the flow of the world. But that's where victory is found!

You'll encounter sharp rungs—such as harsh words spoken by people who are withholding mercy. There will be many other obstacles that tear at your grip. You'll even receive advice from well-intentioned persons on how to jump off or increase comfort while sinking. However, such advice, while sounding good, relies upon self-effort that always fails, because it actually is moving you in the wrong direction. What you need most is to keep constantly climbing up the ladder toward the Lord. It will require that you tilt your head upward, looking to the heavens, instead of looking around or comparing yourself to others. It also means that you must rely upon the Lord for His strength and His direction.

When trying to decipher in which direction you are heading, ask yourself what real desire you have regarding holiness and purity in your innermost being. Openly examine whether you truly want to meet with God and be his friend. If you secretly want to remain in the world because some temporary pleasure has captured your attention, you won't outpace the speed of descent. The ladder won't stay put for you while you are playing the games of the world. Even if you're not actively seeking out impurity, the ladder never stops pulling you down.

The same is true for times you reached new heights, you cannot rest. For instance, a man may be strides ahead of where he was four weeks ago when he began meeting with the Lord through Proven Men's companion *Study* named, *The 12-Week Study to a PROVEN Path to Sexual Integrity*. But the moment he ends his journey of climbing toward and with the Lord, he will begin to lose what he gained. It won't take too long before he is backsliding. That's why you cannot rest upon yesterday's efforts, no matter how noble they were. That's why we don't call our *Study* a 12-week "program." Yet, it's still a good tool for beginning a new lifelong journey of intimacy with and dependency upon the Lord.

Instead of being discontent that the ladder of life is constantly on a downgrade, be excited that the Lord has revealed this knowledge to you and has provided you with His strength to overcome and rise above. Won't you commit the rest of your life to striving for absolute purity as part of your ascension toward the heavenly skies? The Lord is calling you to journey with Him to higher places, into His inner courts and into His very presence.

Carrying Your Cross Daily

Christ said, "If anyone desires to come after me, let him deny himself, and take up his cross daily, and follow me."[146] Do you view the command to pick up your cross daily and follow Christ as some harsh command? Perhaps you even liken it to a contest to see who can withstand the most pain in trying to earn love?

To help you understand this verse, consider that Christ also asked you to "take my yoke upon you."[147] In that passage, the Lord explained that such commands are actually invitations to let Christ carry the load. Here's the full passage:

> *Take my yoke upon you and learn from me, for I am gentle and humble in heart, and you will find rest for your souls. For my yoke is easy and my burden is light.*[148]

When trusting in Christ, the burden doesn't get heavier but actually gets lighter because it's Jesus who is carrying it. Similarly, when you take up the cross, it's Jesus Himself who carries it. Christ is inviting you to join your life with His. This means that you take up the cross, not by carrying it, but by yielding to God. You allow the Lord to supply the power. He provides the direction. He carries the load.

You do, however, need to die to lust for the world and replace it with a longing for the Lord. You must stay in His camp to enjoy His protection and peace. Your will must bend to His, because only one can lead at a time. Start following the Lord and let Him carry the load.

In short, it was Christ's role to pay the punishment for your sin on the cross; it's your role to exchange a worldly life for one hidden in Christ Jesus Himself as you deny self and follow Him. Denying self not only means learning to be humble (the antidote for pride), but happens to be the only place where real relationships with God and others prosper. In other words, created man is to deny self-worth while admitting that Jesus is God and thereby purposefully worshiping and trusting Him in all things. The exchanging of your hands for Christ's involves the same principle of putting down the shovel of self-effort and yielding your life completely to Him.

At first, I was upset that I must pick up my cross daily when I realized that my cross was that I might be tempted to lust every day for the rest of my life. But the more I met with and relied on Christ, the more I was grateful for knowing that my daily cross would be to wake up each day with a fresh commitment that lust and masturbation are not options. I came to enjoy daily putting into practice the six letters of the PROVEN acronym. The more I quickly rejected the temporary pleasures of second looks or lustful fantasies, the easier it got to live without fantasy and masturbation. In fact, it has been over fifteen years since I looked at pornography or masturbated. But that's only because every day I pick up the cross and die to self ... die to selfishness and pride.

Don't Ditch Your Partner

Beware of another lie. Satan will tell you that you don't need any help from a *networking partner*—that you can do it on your own.

Wrong. You need accountability. There are no shortcuts. However, the most frequently skipped PROVEN letter is *"N."* Most men don't want to link up with another man. Many are embarrassed. Others don't know how because they never had a good model. Regardless of the reason, if you skip the *networking* aspect, you'll likely never experience lasting victory. The old nature will sneak back in.

Without the *n*, the word spells "prove." That's a dangerous word in this context because ditching the *N* is the single most common reason why men don't remain living in sexual integrity. Think of it this way, you're saying *prove* it to me that I need the help of another man. That's pride speaking. Remember, pride is the root that keeps sexual sin alive. So, if you aren't willing to swallow your pride, you'll be fighting against God rather than relying on Him. That's a sure fire way to remain in bondage to sin.

At a recent church picnic, a man walked straight to up me and engulfed me in a big hug. Bursting with a smile, he beamed, "I have been clean for three years!" Years before, he had come to a 12-week support group I led with a handful of men trying to lead lives of purity. I remembered clearly how discouraged he had been. He worked at a local college and talked about how defeated he felt because every new day he faced a constant barrage of pretty young women streaming into his workplace. At the time, it felt like more than he could take. When I asked him what had changed, he said the key to his victory was networking. After our support group ended, he had arranged to meet with one of the other men from the group twice a week. They had kept it up for the past three years. Because neither of them ditched *networking*, both had given up pornography (and lust) for as long as they keep networking.

In short, you need accountability. There are no shortcuts. Please, dear brother, link up with another man in *network* accountability. Join the brotherhood of Proven Men. God wants you to realize that you are needy and dependent upon Him. So keep an eternal perspective and trust completely in God to do the healing in your life as He knows best: Alongside another Proven Man.

Comfort Others

Your pain is not in vain. The Lord will use your struggles for His glory. Consider this passage.

> *Praise be to the God and Father of our Lord Jesus Christ, the Father of compassion and the God of all comfort, who comforts us in all our troubles, so that we can comfort those in any trouble with the comfort we ourselves have received from God. For just as the sufferings of Christ flow into our lives, so also through Christ our comfort overflows.*[149]

Did you notice that as a Christian, you're not exempt from experiencing suffering? God warns you in advance that you will suffer. In fact, God likens your difficulties to Christ's sufferings, which He says flow into your life. However, as the sufferings keep flowing into you, they need to be released or you'll grow bitter as you hold in all of your pain. God's perfect plan for refreshing you is by washing out your sufferings (and any bitterness or anger) as you extend comfort and compassion to others.

Do you have a burden for others? As you begin taking the focus off yourself, you'll see great pain in the lives of others. The more you yield to God, the more you experience His divine nature, including His compassion.

God also gives you the privilege of comforting others with the same comfort God granted to you. You had to strive hard to experience sexual integrity. Now God has a plan for you.

There are countless other men who are benchwarmers, many of them in your church, because they don't have a *network partner* to comfort them in the same struggle you face. They're afraid they'll be judged if they tell a Christian man they look at pornography or masturbate.

Will you extend the same comfort to them? Will you step alongside a brother without judging, but gently guiding him or walking the journey together? What a wonderful privilege the Lord has for you—to offer comfort to another man who is hurting, who is trapped in bondage to lust, who is losing the fight for sexual integrity. Your pain is not in vain, but there is more to it than you living in victory. It will actually be a comfort to another man who is facing similar pain. It's time to give back to the Lord by openly reaching out to other men. It's also a part of the *N*.

My dear brother, won't you link with another and invite him to become a Proven Man? Won't you please be open and honest with another about your struggle so you can encourage them and be similarly encouraged?

Consider the Dead Sea

It's a tremendous body of water, which has all of the elements for sustaining abundant life. Yet the sea is dead. It's dead because, unlike all other seas, it's fed by many inlets but has no outlets feeding other waterways. By only permitting incoming water with no out flowing tributaries, it retains heavy quantities of salt and other impurities that kill life.

Your life will be similarly choked with impurity if you merely seek to receive God's blessings without striving alongside others. When you act selfishly you fail to look to the interests of others or extend heartfelt comfort and compassion. As you look out just for yourself or try to hold inside goodness or blessings, you end up stagnating as you restrict your outflow, which causes bitter waters of lust and other sins stemming from selfishness and pride to remain inside your body and soul.

Like a healthy sea, networking is a two-way exchange, keeping both healthy and pure. By looking outside of yourself and linking with a *networking partner,* you accept the Lord's comfort as you allow that comfort and healing to flow through you.[150] As you do, the extension of His comfort outward to others washes out of you the pain of your underlying trials and sufferings. Yet, if you don't extend yourself to others, you bottle up the pain inside. It's that simple. You can be like the Dead Sea and just seek victory from sexual sins for yourself, or, after you start receiving victory you can be a *network partner* for other men that are asking the Lord for help.

Tilt the Mirror Upward

It's a wonderful thing to see others experience victory. Don't let your ability to help others create a sense of pride in you. As you reach out to and comfort others, tilt the mirror upward toward God and off yourself. Don't make it about you. You shouldn't be helping others just so you can receive the praise. You shouldn't be boasting—either by bragging about how pure you are now or how impure you were before. Rather, keep your desire pure for wanting to comfort and serve others. As you do, the reflection they'll see is that of Christ, not you.

The Lord wants to use you as His arms to hold and comfort the hurting. If you want to be used by God in the healing process of others, pray very specifically for the Lord to humble you and to open opportunities to work in other men. Your greatest need is not education or training, but rather to be filled by and to follow the leading of the Holy Spirit. To be used by God, you must know

Him and live a life punctuated by prayer and praise. Therefore, make it your purpose to live out a Proven life; one that seeks God with all of your heart, that yields total control, and lives by His Spirit. Then, you will be complete, stamped PROVEN by God and be ready to serve. What privilege awaits you!

There is no magical formula to the Proven Path for sexual integrity. It's simply a roadmap for living out your Christian life. The key is that all six letters must be included in your daily life. Even the absence of one will thwart you from building or retaining sexual integrity.

Do the 12-Week Daily Study

There's a lot more involved in striving for sexual integrity than reading this book and making a commitment. It takes time to undo backward thinking or habits and build into your life the six letters of the PROVEN acronym. For instance, most men are not used to being open and honest and many need a safe environment to start practicing. That's one reason why we prepared a daily study named, *The 12-Week Study to a PROVEN Path to Sexual Integrity,* which is available through our website (www.ProvenMen.com) or online bookstores. We strongly encourage you to work through it as part of a small group or with a *networking partner.*

At the risk of being overly redundant, remember that refusing to link up with a *network accountability partner* is one of the single most common reasons why a man doesn't break free from sexual sin. Please don't be too proud to tell another man of your struggle and to allow him to step along side of you and even go through our 12-week companion *Study* at the same time. Otherwise, you'll be going it alone and outside of the Lord's healing plan. I know of many men who are now divorced who wish they had taken this admonition sooner, and many more who are still riding a purity roller coaster. I pray and plead with you to include the vital N in PROVEN.

As you get ready to strive forward, be forewarned that our companion *Study* is very intense because shedding sexual sins and building sexual integrity into your life is very intense. It takes much time and effort to get a firm foundation with the fundamentals. Just as each year a professional sports team spends long hours for weeks in spring training going over and over the fundamentals, you need the same time putting the fundamentals into practice. Regardless of the degree of your struggle, you should work through our 12-week companion *Study*. Even if you're a pastor or lay leader with the goal of simply keeping strong your sexual integrity, the *Study* is beneficial. Not only will it strengthen you, but it will help you help others who are just starting to build sexual integrity.

Please remember that the sexual integrity is a lifetime process. After working through our 12-week *Study*, be committed to remaining in Biblical studies and networking for the rest of your life. There's no coasting as a Christian. But, at the same time, don't miss out on the journey with the Lord as you begin aiming for sexual integrity. In other words, don't just try to survive for 12 weeks or 12 months. Take on an *eternal perspective* and purpose to enjoy the process no matter how difficult it is because the Lord will be walking with you at each step along the path.

Victorious in Living

There are way too many headlines today about how our role models, whether a preacher, politician or professional athlete, got caught up in sexual sin and took a tumble. The life of a Proven Man is just the opposite. No, we are not perfect. But it's the direction in which we are heading that makes the difference. We are climbing out of, not into sin. We are striving for sexual integrity, not selfish indulgence.

What about those of us who once chased after these things? Great news! You have now become a Proven Man. My life is a good example. But let me share with you a passage I hold dear that gives me hope and keeps me from thinking my past is a disqualification.

Apostle Paul begins a passage by first warning that those who live selfish lives filled with sexually immorality, idolatry, adultery and other sexual deviant behaviors don't deserve to inherit the Kingdom of God, which literally means they are not going to heaven.[151] In case some of the listeners were thinking of judging, Paul adds that the same goes for anyone who slanders or cheats. Well, which of us never did either of those two things? Even though the passage was talking to Christians, just to make sure the listener was not too busy comparing his life to others instead of focusing on the Lord, Paul rounds out the introduction with: "And that is what some of you *were*." That's right. We *were* in the same camp as those sinners deserving hell.

Now listen to the beauty of the redemption story, which picks up in the next sentence, and should give you hope: "But you were washed, you were sanctified, you were justified in the name of the Lord Jesus Christ and by the Spirit of our God." Yes! That once was me, but not anymore. I am now a Child of God. I don't carry around with me forever the title of former or recovering sex addict. I wear the name Proven Man.

▶ **JOEL: From Addict to Elder**

Fifteen years ago was the last time I looked at pornography or masturbated. Three years after I first truly gave up my secret and shameful ways, I began burning with passion to help other men break free, so I formed my first sexual integrity support group and began writing a study to help others. A year later, the IRS granted me non-profit status for Proven Men Ministries, and I began taking this ministry around the world.

Leading up to that time, my life was being radically transformed. Everyone began noticing a change in me. I was not the same person who argued all the time and had to be right or win at everything. My wife's friends would secretly ask her what happened, hoping there was some formula that they could give to their husbands. Even my church leaders saw a new and Proven Man in me and I am now an elder at my local church.

My stamp of PROVEN was not awarded because of a certain number of days I have not masturbated, but remains based upon a heart that purposes to put into practice each of the six letters of the acronym.

▶ TIM: A New Worldview

Tim no longer believes the lies that he doesn't measure up or is no good. He is so overwhelmed by the love of the Lord that he cannot help but cry during prayer or worship times. Tim gave up self medication of porn, alcohol and masturbating 10 times a day, to spending time meeting with the Lord.

Although it took Tim three times through the *Proven Men Study,* once it took hold, Tim never turned back. Sure, there were the occasional times when the old voice was telling him that he didn't deserve love that led to Tim retreating into masturbation, but Tim quickly ran back to the Lord.

Today, Tim has been leading support groups for more than five years. He is still quick to search out and find men who have low self esteem so he can put his arms around them and share his story and his life.

▶ **STAN: Married and Madly in Love**

Stan has done the unthinkable. He went against the tidal wave of the world and stopped having premarital sex even though he was engaged to be married. It was hard, but it was no longer an option. Only when he was willing to stop being alone with Missy did he begin to win the battles. He also gave up pornography for good.

Stan is glad he suffered through it because he is now married and still madly in love with Missy. By jointly agreeing to put Christ first while dating, the transition to putting Him first while married was much easier. There are so many more battles in marriage that need this type of commitment, that they were glad for the early training.

With a child on the way, Stan is also grateful that he won't be passing down to his children a selfish lifestyle or sexual sins. He trusts God at his word that even though the sins of a selfish man are passed to the third and fourth generation, this cycle can be broken by turning to the Lord and receiving God's mercy and promise of showing love to a thousand generations of those who love and keep God's commandments.[152]

Conclusion and Final Admonition

I am convinced that there is only one Proven Path to sexual integrity. It's based upon completely surrendering your pride and selfishness and replacing it with becoming a needy, dependent servant of the Lord Jesus Christ. In practical terms, it means implementing and testing your life daily upon these six principles, in which you seek to be:

Passionate for God,
Repentant in spirit,
Open and honest,
Victorious in living,
Eternal in perspective, and
Networked with other ***Proven Men.***

It won't be an easy battle. But please never give up because the mark of a Proven Man is not the absence of sin, but how you respond to it.

In my own journey I still face on a daily basis the same temptations common to all men and am susceptible to attack. I am in essence a wounded helper pointing others to the never-ending supply of grace in Jesus. I don't measure my days (or my worth) based on the length of time between sins. Rather, each new day I must make a fresh commitment to holiness and pursuing the Lord.

Therefore, with personal conviction I exhort you in the same manner as the Apostle Peter concluded in his last letter to the church: "Be on guard ... and grow in the grace and knowledge of our Lord and Savior Jesus Christ."[153] Please make my joy complete by joining the brotherhood of Proven Men by being like-minded, having the same love and passion for the Lord and each other, and becoming one in spirit and purpose.

APPENDICES

Passionate for God,

Repentant in spirit,

Open and honest,

Victorious in living,

Eternal in perspective, and

Networking with other *Proven Men.*

Appendix

Why Jesus?

If all you want is to stop a sexual sin you hate, then you don't need this book. If you want to stay in complete control of your life, try behavioral modification techniques. Take a secular psychology class or read self-help books that tell you how to pull yourself up by your own bootstraps and fix everything that's wrong with your life.

The premise of this book is that those techniques will fail. My book exists to humbly share with you exactly what you need. From my own experience and the experience of hundreds of other Proven Men, I can tell you: If you want to live a purposeful and Proven life, you need Jesus.

You'll remain trapped in sexual addiction unless you do two things:

1. Ask Jesus to be your Savior.
2. Give Him permission to be Lord of your *entire* life.

Jesus as Savior

Allow me to explain Jesus in a way you might not have heard.

Many believe that Jesus came to earth to show us how to live a good life. That's not why Jesus came to earth. Yes, Jesus surely did provide the greatest example. But He didn't come here to show you how to live, but to die on the cross and rise again as your Savior.

Jesus was and is God. He is the one who created the world. About 2,000 years ago Jesus left heaven to take the form of a man. Why?

When the Lord created man, He had a divine purpose for an eternal relationship with each one of us. However, the heavenly dwelling of God is absolutely perfect. God says that nothing impure can enter into heaven.[154] That's a huge problem because every one of us has sinned. A single sin makes us imperfect and ineligible to be in heaven. In fact, the Bible is crystal clear that the penalty for a single sin is eternal separation from God.[155]

It's like we are all on death row waiting to be executed. I am sure your mother or father would gladly step in your place to pay your death sentence. But they cannot because they too have sinned and are on death row.

What we all desperately need is for someone not on death row to be willing to take the punishment for us. Of course, that means they would have to live a sinless life. Do you see where this is going? Only God could live a sinless life on earth. That's why Jesus took on flesh 2,000 years ago. Being man and God at the same time, Jesus did not commit a single sin.[156] The good news is that Jesus was willing to lay down His life for yours.

Jesus personally paid the penalty of your sin when He died on the cross. John 3:16 is perhaps the best known verse in the Bible: "For God so loved the world that he gave his one and only Son, that whoever believes in him shall not perish but have eternal life." If you were the only person to have ever lived, Jesus would still have come to earth to die for you. It had to be that way. He loves you and doesn't want you to perish or to go on living without Him as part of your life. In fact, Christ offers you His name and His righteousness to replace your sin-soiled life.

By living a perfect life, Jesus became an acceptable sacrifice and substitute for your sin. Then he conquered death by rising from the grave and returned to heaven. Now, when the death sentence is handed down for your sins, Jesus stands in your place—provided you have accepted His free gift of forgiveness occurring when you ask the Lord to permanently dwell in your heart. That way, when you die and the punishment of death must be paid, Jesus who lives in you, has already paid the penalty in full.

What do you need to do to ask Jesus to be your Savior? The Bible says, "If we confess our sins, He is faithful and just and will forgive us our sins and purify us from all unrighteousness."[157] He won't reject you. Everyone who turns to Jesus and believes in Him become children of God and therefore inherit eternal life in heaven.[158] This includes you and me, but you must personally ask for and accept the free gift of forgiveness.

If you turn to Jesus and accept His shed blood as the perfect sacrifice and substitute for your penalty, you're no longer considered impure no matter what bad things you've done or will do. God the Father will not reject you because His Son, who now lives in you, already paid the full penalty of death for all your sins.

Right now, go to God with a surrendered heart. You'll be asking Jesus, who paid the death penalty that was due to you, to forgive you and to enter your heart. Ask Him for His grace and mercy. He wants to give it to you.

Salvation

To ask Jesus into your heart and accept God's righteousness, pray something like this:

God, I know that I am a sinner and deserve death. I know that Jesus is God and that He died on the cross to rescue me from the penalty of my sin. Please forgive me. I receive the free gift of eternal life, which comes solely from the perfect sacrifice of Jesus Christ for my sin. I pray and ask you, Jesus, to come into my heart right now and to make it your permanent home. Take total control of my life. I choose to follow you and turn away from sin, including my former lifestyle. Thank you for loving me and forgiving me. I commit to following you forever. In your precious name, Jesus, I pray these things. Amen.

If you prayed this prayer with your heart, then congratulations! You're my eternal brother in Christ. You're free from the power of death. Jesus now permanently lives in you, and you're God's child.

Jesus as Lord

It's now time to daily make Jesus Lord of your life. That's the key to sexual integrity.

You've taken a very important step. You've realized that you can't win the battle on your own. You've probably tried many times and failed, but you're finally on the right track. You see, your battle is not about using more of your own power or even about overcoming bad influences. Instead, it's a spiritual battle. In fact, the Bible teaches that "our struggle is not against flesh and blood, but against the rulers, against the authorities, against the powers of this dark world and against the spiritual forces of evil in the heavenly realms."[159]

The only way to stop being a slave to sin, such as pornography, is to rely on Jesus Christ. These are more than just words. When you need forgiveness, power, and strength, you go to the source of forgiveness, power, and strength: Jesus. His power is available to you, so turn to and yield your entire life to Him.

Now the journey begins, but you never travel alone! A wonderful by-product of having an intimate relationship with God is victory over sins, including sexual immorality. Jesus desires to take control of your life and lead you in His holy and pure ways. The power of the Holy Spirit is ready, willing, and more than able to lead you victoriously if you let Him, but you must want to love and serve God more than your former selfish and prideful ways. You need to start hating sin because it blocks your relationship with Jesus Christ.

Making Jesus Lord over your daily life is what being a Proven Man is all about. Each day you wake up you give control to the Lord. Throughout the day, you test your thoughts and actions against the six PROVEN letters:

> **P**assionate for God,
> **R**epentant in spirit,
> **O**pen and honest,
> **V**ictorious in living,
> **E**ternal in perspective, and
> **N**etworked with other ***Proven Men.***

Plan to work through our 12-week companion *Study* named *The 12-Week Study to a PROVEN Path to Sexual Integrity,* to learn how to live out a Proven life. It's a journey you never have to take alone because you're part of the family of God and a fellow Proven Man.

Passionate for God,
Repentant in spirit,
Open and honest,
Victorious in living,
Eternal in perspective, and
Networking with other *Proven Men.*

Appendix

What about Masturbation?

The Bible doesn't mention masturbation. But before you decide that "no news is good news," I would ask you to think about this: The Bible doesn't mention arson, child abuse, drug-trafficking, forgery, pornography, or vandalism either. Does that give you free reign to sell cocaine on the corner or demolish your hotel room when you're on vacation?

The Lord gives us guiding or life principles that require us to constantly test everything, including the Scriptures and our own hearts. That's because God wants you to meet with Him daily to wrestle with life issues. Masturbation raises a lot of life issues.

I want you to make a decision for yourself about whether or when masturbation is healthy or potentially harmful. Let's start the discussion about a few of the life issues it raises, so you can wrestle with them further in your own conversations with God.

Is Masturbation a Form of Adultery?

One of the main Bible verses used to support the notion that masturbation might be sinful is this: "You have heard that it was said, 'Do not commit adultery.' But I tell you that anyone who looks at a woman lustfully has already committed adultery with her in his heart."[160] It's time for you to examine your thought life as a prelude to or during masturbation.

This isn't saying you can never have any sexual thoughts. Remember the time when you were 16 years old and you spent hours rehearsing your first kiss? An innocent, barely sexual thought like that is not tinged with lust. Fond memories of having sex with your wife and enjoying the afterglow are fine, too. Marital sex is condoned by God. The real danger lies in giving our minds permission to engage in lust.

Lust can be a monster that gets out of control. If you think about it, when a man habitually invents fantasies about women in sexual ways, he trains himself to dehumanize people by stealing their images as visual aides for his own self-centered use.[161] He effectively treats the imaginary women as unpaid prostitutes.[162]

This was me. I was constantly looking for opportunities to engage in lust. At every corner I looked both ways hoping for a pretty woman to stare at. I made it a practice of storing up images throughout the day so I could use them to fuel a nightly routine of sexual fantasies culminating in masturbation. Of course, I rationalized it by pretending that the imaginary women in such fantasies were willing, consenting adults who were pleased to fulfill my every fantasy. I also convinced myself that there was no harm in indulging these fantasies, because there was no real person involved.

The *lust* was the problem. Masturbation was a convenient means of expressing and sustaining it. This is exactly the type of lust Christ warned us about.

Consider Ryan, a 17-year-old senior in high school. Although many of his friends regularly emailed or texted each other pornographic pictures or websites, Ryan didn't join in. He had made a purity vow, so he was careful with his eyes. He had built many good practices into his life, such as reading the Bible daily, going to church on Sundays, and attending Fellowship of Christian Athletes meetings every week. But despite his good intentions, Ryan's adolescent hormones were in overdrive. His convictions meant that he couldn't have sex until he was married. That could be years away! Meanwhile, he woke with an erection many mornings and had to take a long cold shower to ignore it without incident. At least once a week his hormones kicked in and he would dwell on sex. No matter what he did, the clock was ticking. At times, the physical need for release overcame him and he succumbed to masturbation.

Most of us have been there. And considering the developmental phase of adolescent boys and girls, it's harder to determine whether or when Ryan and other teens cross the line of sexual integrity when they masturbate.

What we do know is that lust often begins with your eyes. You may have heard it said that your eyes are the gateway to your soul. I agree. You can tell so much about a person by looking them in the eyes. Your eyes express your emotions and tell the world how you feel.

But the eyes also influence who you are and what you do. The Bible states it this way:

The eye is the lamp of the body. If your eyes are good, your whole body will be full of light. But if your eyes are bad, your whole body will be full of darkness.[163]

Whatever you allow in through your eyes finds its way into the mind. If you look upon sexual images every day, you'll end up dwelling on them and causing your heart to start yearning.

Whenever I had undressed women with my eyes, the images were so enticing that I wanted to replay the images again and again. Like a porn video, I soon started adding the flimsiest story lines: A well-dressed woman in a business suit would stroll past me with apparent indifference, but in my fantasy, when she reached the corner, she glanced back ... making it clear she wanted to have sex. My heart began wanting—no; my heart began *lusting* for sex. It was just a matter of time before my body was desperate for sexual release.

In fact, as soon as the fantasy started I knew I would later masturbate. That was the whole point. It was part of the ritual. Because of the sexualization of our culture, I was constantly surrounded by unnaturally beautiful, seductive women, often scantily dressed and leering at me provocatively from movie posters, magazine covers, soap commercials, ads for everything from socks to lingerie. Any one of those images might stick in my mind and turn into the titillating fantasy of a woman—any one of them—who saw me and lingered, just long enough to touch my arm, to loosen her blouse, to slip me her phone number or to pull me into the stairwell for a quick tryst.

That's why I ask men what they looked at or dwelt upon in the days or hours leading up to masturbation. It's important to find out the condition of a man's eyes and heart before he masturbated. If he was filling his eyes and mind with sexual ideas all day, that activity prompted his need to masturbate. And stopping that activity is the best way for him to intervene in time to avoid giving way to masturbation.

It's not just your imagination: Our culture does engulf us with constant sexual stimuli. "Sex sells" has been the motto of advertising from its inception. As far back as 1871, Pearl Tobacco used naked women to sell tobacco. A few years later, when Duke & Sons became the leading cigarette brand by inserting trading cards with sexually provocative starlets in every pack, it was clear that sex could sell just about anything.

So you are not alone in finding this barrage of sexual images stimulating. That's an almost universal reaction. But if you want to be a Proven Man in a daily relationship with God instead, you have to put Him first.

When men tell me they have masturbated in secret in the stalls of public restrooms or the privacy of their own showers as a result of a barrage of sexual images they couldn't avoid, I reassure them and help them map out a game plan. You may not be able to avoid provocative images entirely. Women are everywhere. Ads selling products via sex are everywhere. But you can interrupt the urge to dwell on the images or let them morph into fantasies that quickly raise the urge for release. It's much harder to resist masturbation once it has gotten to that point.

Assuming your desire to serve God as an integrity driven Proven Man is genuine, you will make your life much easier if you nip your urges in the bud. If you come across yet another movie ad with that same hot starlet who seems to keep cropping up everywhere, look away. Change the subject in your mind.

Even if an attractive woman in the elevator brushes up against you deliberately, why not stare at the ground or start a chirpy conversation in a tone so far removed from sex that it squelches the idea for both of you on the spot. Whatever you do, don't entertain the invitation to focus on lust.

Of course, in addition to these strategies, be sure to start an interesting conversation with God. Ask for His help. Turn your focus to Him, not to selfish thoughts.

Make it your constant strategy to avoid the natural tendency to linger over potentially sexual encounters. You are a Proven Man. And again, you're not alone.

Every Proven Man in America is struggling with exactly the same barrage of sexual stimuli that you are. When all else fails, remember: If they can do it, so can you.

Is Masturbation a Form of Coveting?

Anything that diverts you away from God is wrong. To me, that explains why masturbation is not even addressed in the Bible. The Lord ultimately wants you to live a daily Proven life in wholehearted devotion to Him. That's the ultimate goal. Nothing else—certainly not a distracting focus on avoiding masturbation—should interrupt your communion with Him.

The Bible does list other sexual sins to avoid, but masturbation isn't in the list. It could be because it is not always brought on by sexual stimuli. Orgasm relaxes every muscle in your body and restores your peace of mind. Lust is not always the motivation. That's why we must also test our actions and attitudes by other categories.

When you're under stress, you may feel an urge to masturbate as a relief. Maybe you are angry for being wrongfully accused or overlooked for a promotion. A frequent trigger for a husband to turn to masturbation is a fight with his wife. Tension, anger, frustration, or any feeling that something is unfair often gives way to masturbation. Because it's fun and entertaining, it can also be used as a response to simply feeling tired, bored or lonely. But simply being driven by a non-sexual motive doesn't end the masturbation sin inquiry.

The Tenth Commandment says "do not covet,"[164] which means not to envy or longingly desire something which belongs to another. It's all about craving something you don't have. Yet, not every desire is sinful. It's not wrong to desire a job, car, or a spouse. But, your heart can quickly start to covet. When you go there, it doesn't take much to add masturbation into the mix. Why is that?

As you wrestle with God about whether coveting is part of the reason why you turn to masturbation, consider what Oswald Chambers said: "The core of all sin is the belief that God is not good." Often, when a man turns to masturbation, he is really telling God that He's wrong or that He made a mistake. Instead of waiting for God to take care of things, the man is acting on his own behalf and meeting his own needs. It may sound like one of these petulant statements:

> God is holding out something good from me, so I need to get it myself.
> God was wrong in saying sex is for marriage only, so I can masturbate.
> God doesn't understand my needs, so I must take care of myself.
> God gave me the wrong spouse!
> God gave me too high a sex drive, so I have to masturbate.
> I can do a better job running my own life than God.

Failing to believe that God is good and can be trusted with your life can give rise to a perceived need for fantasy or the release of masturbation. For some, they don't trust that God alone can meet their true needs.[165] Others stopped believing that God actually provides a way out of temptation[166] or they cannot accept that He can keep them from falling as they turn to and trust Him.[167] Frequently, those who chase fantasy are deciding for themselves what is right and coveting after things that God did not intend for them—guided only by their own human desires.

Soon after Dan got married, his wife began withdrawing sexually. She had been sexually abused as a child and painful memories haunted her each time her husband approached her sexually. Sadly, Dan's wife limited sex to once every three months. Surely, if any man had a good reason to masturbate is was Dan. Because his wife was unbending, his pastor gave Dan permission to masturbate—*as long as he only thought about his wife.*

When I met Dan, it had been a year since he was given the green light to masturbate. I asked him if was glad he masturbated. He sadly looked me in the eyes and said, "No." He explained that it really made no physical difference beyond the act itself. He quickly added that masturbation only fueled a desire for sex. He began craving it more and more. He took his eyes off the Lord and became increasingly discontent with a marriage that had forced him to masturbate alone, rather than enjoying a normal sex life with his wife. He began resenting his wife, eventually even hating her.

It took awhile, but Dan himself made a choice to stop masturbating. Instead he focused on clinging even harder each day to the Lord. Even though his situation did not change much, Dan is more content and at peace now than he was in the year he masturbated.

What Does Your Conscience Say?

God has provided you with a compass to guide you in determining whether masturbation violates your own sexual integrity: Your conscience. It grieves God when your conscience is screaming for you not to do something and you choose to do it anyway. If you cannot do something with a clear conscience, you sin by doing it.[168]

Many psychologists suggest that the guilt you feel after masturbating is nothing more than the result of societal pressure. They claim that if your parents or church leaders didn't tell you that masturbation was wrong, you wouldn't feel guilty. This isn't totally true. The Holy Spirit also convicts a believer's heart and soul, which often leads to feelings of guilt or shame.

When Larry was eleven, his mom found pornography on his computer. She told him it was dirty and evil. She ordered him to stop looking at it. Larry was mortified and made sure his mom would never find it again. Larry kept looking at the photos and masturbating, but after that time, Larry always felt shame when he masturbated. He vowed to keep it a secret to his grave.

A few years later, Larry's mom read an article about masturbation and casually told him that she believed that masturbation was just something kids did before they got married. At first, Larry felt a sense of relief. His mom was basically telling him that it was okay to masturbate. That night Larry was glad to go to bed early so he could masturbate. In fact, he began masturbating every day.

Yet even though his mom had given her blessing, Larry never fully felt peace. It was like he was putting on "God blinders" each time he began his masturbation ritual, but that didn't stop him. Ultimately, masturbation was a regular part of his life, a practice he carried forward into marriage.

Merely because someone else tells you something is not a sin doesn't mean you can shut off your conscience so you can engage in that activity. Don't keep searching for someone to tickle your ears with what you want to hear.[169] Ask God to speak to you. The Lord has lots to say to those who want to turn to, listen to, and obey Him.[170]

There is a danger, however, in solely measuring sin by whether you think something is sin. Just because you don't feel guilty doesn't mean that something is not sinful.

In fact, the Bible says we can deceive ourselves through repeatedly ignoring His warnings and giving ourselves over to the lust of the world.[171] Besides, you simply cannot ignore the elements of lust or coveting, which are sins that must be repented or they will create a dividing wall between you and the Lord.

Another Thing to Consider

Another issue comes not from the Bible, but from the hearts of women. Most women don't want their husbands (or boyfriends) masturbating.

If this is an issue for her and you keep it up anyway, it may mean you have to *lie* to your wife or girlfriend in order to masturbate. Whatever you think about masturbation, it's clear that lying or cheating is not a recipe for a healthy relationship.

Women know all too well that self-sex (which is really what masturbation means) is more about "sex" than "intimacy," and women long for intimacy. They're rightfully afraid that they can never measure up to your sexual fantasies and they worry even more when you are treating sex simply as sex.

Things also get blurry when "sex" is viewed solely as a physical activity. If that were all there was to it, sex need not be reserved just for marriage.

Let's face it, sexual acts feel good in a wide variety of settings—with or without intimacy. However, God did design sexual activities as a function of marriage.

Sex can be far more than a good feeling between two consenting adults. In marriage, sex can be a unifying experience that joins a couple as one in spirit.[172] This intimate expression of love involves and solidifies a total commitment unique to a marriage where divorce or giving of oneself to another is prohibited. You're to be permanently joined and totally committed to your mate in the deepest bonds of intimacy, highlighted by sexual intimacy. As you accept this, you'll better see how masturbation often fights against the ideal of sexual intimacy between spouses.

Singles Face Big Challenges

My heart aches especially for the single man waiting for marriage. It's hard to live in this sex-based body without masturbating. Nearly every Christian man has masturbated. A large portion of men masturbate daily, weekly or monthly.

Yet what is the biggest lie of Satan to single men? *Your struggle with sex will go away when you get married, so you may as well masturbate now to hold you over.*

In truth, it doesn't go away. The patterns you develop as a single man carry over into marriage. Both Tim and I continued to masturbate regularly during marriage. In fact, 60 percent of Christian men continue to regularly masturbate into marriage.

The bigger issue is how masturbation affects your relationship with the Lord. If you know it's sinful for you and keep doing it, you'll be caught up in a downward spiral that leads you ever further away from the Lord. As you feel guilt and shame, you hide and may even try to medicate yourself with the very thing that caused the shame by escaping into fantasy and masturbation.

Stan and Missy were dating during college. Most dates ended up with passionate kissing and groping. After Stan got back to his apartment, his hormone levels were so high he would masturbate to relieve the pressure. He would either replay in his mind the evening or try to empty his mind just to get the release. Stan figured that it was better this way than to press Missy for sex.

Clearly masturbation wasn't the main issue for Stan. He was fueled by his hormones. He knew Missy wanted to remain a virgin, but he didn't want to wait. Eventually, Stan pressed Missy to second base. Within a few weeks he rounded third base. Then one night he crossed home plate.

Stan's masturbation hadn't protected Missy's virginity, nor had it quenched the sexual fire in Stan. Masturbation was just one stop along the way. Stan stoked his urges by constantly thinking about and pursuing sexual activities with Missy. Had he stopped those thoughts before they rushed to a fever pitch, he may have been able to go without sex for years until they were able to walk down the altar together, a sanctified couple in God's eyes.

What about Married Men?

Sometimes men ask me, "Surely, it's okay for a married man to go into a room by himself to think about his wife as he masturbates, right?"

Let me ask this: Are you really thinking about your wife?

First of all, I know how easy it is to claim you are thinking about your wife, but I can tell you: God knows the difference.

Secondly, the woman in your mind as you masturbate may be cast in the image of your wife, but isn't it really a pseudo wife—the wife you wish you had instead of the one who is not in the mood? Isn't she an imaginary version of your wife—the wife you didn't bother pursuing for sexual intimacy for any number of reasons?

The chances are that you're engaging in self-sex and justifying it because you can conjure up a visual image of her, tailored to meet your own needs and desires without hesitation. That makes it hard to argue that you really are thinking about your wife.

The other potential problem may be that as a married man masturbating instead of having sex with your wife is that, when you pursue self-sex, you often rob your wife of your sexual energy. If you cannot fulfill your intimacy duties as a husband because you have been masturbating, it will not matter to her whether you have been imagining having sex with her or not. You have been going for immediate gratification, rather than waiting to include her. If her true needs are still unmet, it will be clear that you have been putting your own needs first, not hers. Consider that.

Decision Time

It's now up to you to wrestle with the topic of masturbation.

There's no doubt that masturbation is addictive and habit form-ing, but also feels good and releases tension. It certainly teeters on the edge of lust and only you know if it crosses that line. You also are the one to weigh whether guilt and shame associated with it causes you to hide from God or if it keeps areas of your heart off limits from a wife or future wife.

Talk to the Lord about it. He wants to hear from you.

How Can You Stop Masturbating?

The truth is that it's hard to stop masturbating! In fact, you're not strong enough to win this battle on your own. You need God's grace and power.[173]

It will likely be the biggest battle you face.

Just how big of a trial will it be? It reminds me of the verse: "In your struggle against sin, you have not yet resisted to the point of shedding your blood."[174] In other words, resisting to the point of shedding blood is the type of strength you need. Don't shy away from this or another trial. God said that trials are useful for developing perseverance and perfecting you.[175] In fact, you'll need perseverance in marriage too!

You'll probably have times where you stumble. But you can be victorious.

As you face your battles, remember this: God is interested in a daily relationship with you. He wants you to understand that you are a created being (whom He loves) and that you're dependent upon Him. In this process, the Lord wants to train you in many things—things that will transform you more and more into a Proven Man.[176] For instance; He wants you to learn to control your body[177] and to learn self-control.[178]

The Lord also wants you to learn the art of fleeing from temptation and sin.[179] It's a valuable lesson that will perfect your life. In the area of masturbation, one of the first things you will need to do is to flee by not allowing inputs, such as pornography or second looks. You'll also need to end your fantasy life and stop thinking of ways to gratify the worldly passions.[180] That means not dwelling on sex. It also means avoiding or abstaining from triggers that lead to masturbation.[181]

In addition, the Lord wants you to renew your mind.[182] You've already seen too much of the world. It's time to fix your eyes on the Lord. Part of renewing your mind is protecting your eyes. In short, although the hardest, the first option is often the best one—to eliminate outside sexual stimulus so that the hormones can dissipate instead of using masturbation as the release. Combine this with purposing to include all six aspects of the PROVEN acronym and you'll soon be living a Proven life.

Actions You Might Take

Although there are no set steps or programs to follow, if you want to stop it's important that you begin by making a *heart shift*. You must take the focus off yourself and your circumstances and put it on the Lord. That's the key. It begins with a firm commitment to the Lord. It also requires a commitment that masturbation is *not an option*, period. It also means resolving to do *whatever it takes* to fulfill that commitment. Only then will you taste lasting victory.

You also need to become a doer, not merely a hearer of God's word.[183] We suggest that you work through our companion *Study* named, *The 12-Week Study to a PROVEN Path to Sexual Integrity*. You'll need the 12 weeks it takes to go through it partly because it takes four weeks to end a habit and four weeks to replace it with a new one. The main reason for using the *Study,* however, is that you need specific training in the area of sexual integrity, such as how to put into place practical measures, including the three Rs for dealing with temptations.

Finally, it's important to attend a sexual integrity support group or otherwise enlist a networking partner. You simply cannot win this battle on your own.

A Word of Caution about Guilt and Shame

I wish we were talking face-to-face so you would see my heart. In support groups, I am gentle and understanding when a man mentions that he has masturbated during the week.

I don't judge a man who masturbates nor do I hold it against him. I encourage and comfort those who struggle just as the Lord comforts instead of condemns me when I have setbacks. I also keep bringing the issue back to the need for living out a daily Proven life. Again, God is interested in a daily relationship with you, not merely that you cut out a certain sin.

Please hear me; I don't intend to make you feel guilt or shame. I know that guilt and shame doesn't bring you closer to God, but will lead you away in a downward spiral.

Ironically, when a person feels guilty about masturbation, he wants to hide. The most common escape mechanism is fantasy and masturbation, which fuels more guilt or shame, leading to more hiding in masturbation, and so on. Therefore, to shame you would defeat the very purpose of this book and my ministry.

I was addicted to masturbation for 20 years. It nearly cost me everything. It was also the hardest thing in the world for me to give up. I want to spare you the pain and missed opportunities occurring while you hide in a make believe world centered upon fantasy or masturbation.

There is a spiritual battle raging around and over you. The devil is your enemy. He will do anything to keep you steeped in guilt and shame so that you don't enjoy intimacy with the Lord. Don't allow him to keep you a bench warming Christian by believing any of his lies.

The good news is that the Lord loves you unconditionally. God's love is not dependent upon how often you do or don't masturbate or commit a sin. He wants your daily friendship. He wants you to discuss your struggles with Him. He wants you to turn to Him in everything. God is in the business of redeeming and restoring, not rejecting anyone who comes to Him.

Every moment you shrink away in self-condemnation or guilt you're playing into the hand of Satan. The devil wants you hiding outside of God's camp and thinking you're unworthy. But that's not God's way, nor the way of a Proven Man.

Please don't live a defeated life by beating yourself up if you masturbate. Reread Chapter 8 in this book discussing *setbacks*— noting that we all experience them and that they don't remove your Proven Men stamp.

Stay in the game. Keep running back to the Lord and keep referring back to the PROVEN acronym to remind you on how to live and whom to live for:

Passionate for God,
Repentant in spirit,
Open and honest,
Victorious in living,
Eternal in perspective, and
Networked with other *Proven Men.*

Finally, remember that the mark of a Proven Man is not the absence of masturbation, but how you respond anytime you have a setback. God's love for you (or your worth) is not based upon whether or when you last masturbated.

Passionate for God,
Repentant in spirit,
Open and honest,
Victorious in living,
Eternal in perspective, and
Networking with other *Proven Men.*

Appendix

What do I tell my Wife or Fiancée?

When I first told my wife that I was addicted to masturbation and accompanying sexual fantasy that eventually progressed in an emotional affair, my wife was devastated. She felt as betrayed as if I'd had a physical extramarital affair. Her security was shaken to the core. Any feeling of being cherished disappeared. She didn't feel as if she had a true marriage. I wasn't sure if I had lost her for good, let alone whether I might ever win her trust again.

Fortunately, I did some things right that helped me rebuild a new life with her and replace the pretend marriage I had been living on my terms with the one God intended for both of us. Specifically:

- I did not wait until I got caught.
- I had a game plan.
- I was resolved that living a secret life was no longer an option.

By the time we spoke, I had already decided I would do whatever it took to put to death pornography, sexual fantasy and masturbation. To guard against repeating the same sins over and over, I knew I needed a plan for living a Proven life as a Godly husband. When I spoke with my wife, the plan was already in place. My resolve was evident in the manner of my confession. I vowed to fight for her and for our marriage. I didn't make excuses. My confession was from my heart. I focused on her needs and included her in the healing process.

Don't Wait Until You Get Caught

Sin will always find you out. No matter how good you think you are at hiding, you will eventually get caught. Whether you confess before or after you get caught can make a big difference because whenever someone gets caught the belated confession rings hollow. It's much harder to rebuild trust when you have only stopped looking at pornography because you got caught. On the other hand, taking the step to expose your own sin can demonstrate you really do want to change.

Even if you get caught first, there's still hope. The real issue is that secrets kill a marriage. It means you must daily continue to live out a lie. You must keep hiding part of yourself from your wife. Trust me, your wife knows something is wrong or missing in your marriage. She may not know right away that your mistresses are the women in your pornography or the mental images in your sexual fantasies, but she knows you're not 100 percent loving and cherishing her.

Here's the deal. If you have a secret fantasy life, right now you're killing your marriage. The only question is whether it will die a slow or quick death. If you keep your secret life hidden, your marriage will die a slow death, since you can never reveal the real you and you'll always be withholding something from your wife. That marriage will be unfulfilling, rocky and filled with pain. Eventually your wife will probably file for divorce because you're always distant from her. In any event, you'll be slowly smothering her and your marriage.

On the other hand, if you confess to your wife your unfaithful heart, your wife may throw you out of the house that night and file for divorce—or … just maybe … your confession could be the start of an honest marriage. As harsh as it may sound, the risk of a quick death is better than a slow and agonizing death. That's because confession is the only path that leaves open the possibility that your wife will forgive you and work with you to build the real and vibrant marriage you never had.

It's this simple: You must be open and honest to have a real marriage. You must let her inside the real you. You must confess to her your secret battle with pornography or other forms of false intimacy. From there, true repentance is the only doorway to building your new marriage. As you put into practice the six disciplines of a Proven life, you have the best chance of rebuilding trust.

Develop a Game Plan

Before talking to your wife or fiancée, begin to develop a game plan. You need to do this for two reasons. First, simply promising to try harder won't usher in lasting change. It's time to develop a Proven game plan, as outlined in this book. Second, it's a good idea to share your game plan with your wife when you tell her the bad news so that she can see a glimmer of hope in the process.

There are three components of this initial game plan. First, read or plan to read this book and commit to working through *The 12-Week Study to a PROVEN Path to Sexual Integrity*. This book provides you with an outline of the healing path so you better understand the process when you discuss your game plan with your wife, and working through the *12-Week Study* will equip you for making lasting change.

Second, plan to put an Internet filter on your computer and smart-telephone, as well as channel or time restrictions on your television. Although, as explained in this book, setting boundaries alone won't result in victory, but it sends the immediate message to your wife that you're serious.

Third, be committed to establishing a *network partner*. Promise to tell another man about your struggles and ask him to regularly walk along side of you. As part of this networking process, plan to sign up for the free service where every website you visit gets emailed to your network partner. More importantly, plan to meet weekly with your network partner. Your wife will be glad to know that you have a good influence in your life, and the fact that you told another man your darkest secrets also reinforces that you are serious about changing and willing to take difficult but necessary steps.

What to tell your Wife

It's time to have the talk. Be sure it's in a quite place (not a restaurant). Allow sufficient time to go through all of these things with her.

Being open and honest is key. You need to confess your sins specifically, letting her know every type or category of activities and the frequency of your engagement with them. For instance, you'll need to tell her if you looked at pornography, if you masturbated, if you texted or called other women, if you had sex with anyone, if you called sex lines, if you visited chat rooms, etc. Yes, if you had an affair with someone, she should be told their name.

You should not tell her the details of every impure thought, such as every woman you ever lusted after and what you were thinking. It isn't that she doesn't have a right to know this information, but the details will only hurt her needlessly. If your description is too graphic, it will detract from the main issue. What you want your wife to understand is the scope and magnitude of the problem. Even though she may ask for more details, keep in mind that those imagines will eventually come back to torture her and needlessly add to her pain.

When I confessed to my wife that I regularly masturbated and lusted after women, she asked me to tell her every woman of whom I'd had a lustful thought. I calmly looked her in the eyes and told her I agreed that she had a right to know, but I wanted her to think about whether she really needed that kind of detail, since I believed it would torture her later.

Instead, I reiterated that I had a game plan and network accountability partner in place and would tell him those types of details. I also told her that it was many women and said I would tell her the details, but asked her to consider whether she really needed to know or was just curious. On reflection, she agreed that it was better not to know.

It was clear from my confession that my mind was filled with thousands of images and fantasies and that it was an addiction in need of help. In fact, I confessed the emotional affair I had with one of her friends by name and gave her the basic information so that she knew the full extent of the affair. She is still glad today not to have been told every small detail, since she would have inevitably played them over and over in her mind.

During those same discussions, I told my wife that I was committed to her, the Lord and our marriage. I told her that I no longer wanted to live this secret life. We discussed how it was more important for me to be open and honest in my relationship with her than for me to either pretend to be sin-free or hide the truth. My wife needed to understand that I would not be perfect or never have a setback, but I was committed to change and to being open.

Like my wife, your wife has a choice. To be part of the solution means that she must first know the scope of the problem and then purpose to have patience and understanding.

One potential burden is the risk that a wife will threaten to leave if you ever have a setback, such as looking at pornography again. Even if she makes this threat in anger or out of hurt, you must avoid the temptation to keep lying and concealing your struggles. You simply cannot live that way anymore. As for me and other Proven Men, we would still risk it all in order to finally have an open and honest relationship.

I told my wife that I needed her to give me the freedom to be honest and to include her in the healing process. She needed to understand that a lifetime of backward thinking won't just change overnight. It helped for her to talk to other wives that had gone through this and to even read books like this one to understand sexual addiction and what a healing path looks like. As scary as it sounds, it's important for you to give her permission to talk to other women.

We also agreed that she would not be my accountability partner. We knew that this would only cause more distrust and hurt. It would cause her to be more of a mother than a wife. Therefore, we reached an understanding that I wouldn't tell her of every lustful thought I had, but would tell her if I ever looked at pornography or masturbated. I would tell my *network partner* of my thought life. Of course, I did agree to allow her access to my accounts, for the reasons discussed above. It provided a good compromise that allowed her to not feel the need to be the accountability partner. I also committed to never being alone with a woman. That meant never going to lunch alone with a female co-worker. That would be non-negotiable.

Each conversation a husband has with his wife will look different. You will likely have several follow-up conversations as the reality sinks in. Stay the course. Be willing to live out all six elements of a Proven life as you include her in the process and rebuild her trust. If you stumble after the initial talk, you will go through a similar process of not waiting to get caught, having a game plan, and having an open conversation with her.

Singles: What to tell your Girlfriend or Fiancée

If you're single, you need to tell your girlfriend or fiancée of your addiction or struggles with pornography or lust prior to getting married. You should not discuss this on your first date, but you should have this discussion prior to asking her to marry you. In fact, you must tell her before you get married or she will feel betrayed, even tricked into marriage. It will be hard for her to forgive you once she eventually learns of your divided heart.

You should be guided by the same principles in this chapter regarding having a game plan, including a *network partner*, and sharing enough details so that she grasps the full magnitude of the issue. Finally, your fiancée should read this book and especially the next chapter, and have the freedom to talk to other women.

Conclusion

Secrets are your enemy and will keep you forever in bondage to sin. Telling your wife or fiancée is one of the hardest parts of the process, but so necessary because openness is one of the six key elements to living out a Proven life.

Passionate for God,
Repentant in spirit,
Open and honest,
Victorious in living,
Eternal in perspective, and
Networking with other *Proven Men.*

Appendix  D

Words for Wives

A Wife's Perspective (The Author's Wife)

As a feeling-oriented woman, it's hard for me to put my feelings aside. In the face of this betrayal, I have to admit that a protective part of me was screaming, "Run! Give up on this marriage!"

As hard as it is not to run or give up in the face of such betrayal, we must never lose sight of the fact that the two greatest commands given by our precious Lord and Savior are to "love the Lord your God with all your heart, with all your soul, and with all your mind" and to "love your neighbor as yourself." (Matthew 22:36-40.)

You might be wondering how you can love a husband who has betrayed you. It's important to remember that all marriages go through rough times. Marriage is a proving ground and perfector of our faith. Whatever else happens, it's important to continually keep a God-focused life.

Remember that, as much as God loves you, you're just as depraved as the next human being (including your husband). We all are sinners. We all fall short in the eyes of a perfectly holy God.

As women, we tend to focus on the person causing us pain and lose sight of God in the process. When we focus on the sins of others, we cannot see what God is trying to show us about Himself. Therefore, we must purpose to be passionate for the Lord because to live at peace and have contentment in this world regardless of circumstances requires that we have an intimate, daily relationship with Jesus. He will enable you to love and even trust again.

Next, there is hope for restoration. God changes hearts and lives. But please know this: You cannot do it for your husband—nor are you expected to! If you try to take on too much responsibility, then you enable him to stay in the place where he is at instead of him relying on God for the strength he needs. On the other hand, if you're too hands off and see this as solely his problem, you won't be able to see what God can and wants to do in your life and in your husband's life through this struggle.

Certainly you want a man who goes after God's heart ... a PROVEN Man. But don't expect or demand a PERFECT man. God wants to restore people, but He takes them at a pace they can handle. Your privilege as a wife is to be a helpmate. Help means just that, "help." You're not to take care of it for him, nor are you to ignore or refuse any role in the healing process. This frees you up to let God work in your husband's life and in your marriage.

I know that your pain is real. But please guard against the fantasy that your marriage (or your life) should be pain-free or that this pain is worse than other trials and struggles you will have on earth. Yes, marriage is painful. Yes, marriage is hard work, but marriage also is a wonderful and purposeful institution sanctioned by God.

It's better to know the truth, as difficult as it may be to hear it. Beyond your husband's confession, there is another truth to face: There is no guarantee that—even if you do everything right—your husband will stop. Instead, your anchor of hope must be in God and the faithfulness of God—not your husband—and not based upon the outcome to this struggle.

With all of this in mind, there are some suggestions I would like to make based on what God has shown me because of His desire for me to grow and know Him deeper.

It's a "We Problem"

As for all issues in marriage, your husband's fight for sexual integrity is a "we problem" not a "he problem." You should be actively involved in the process. Consider reading books written by wives who have gone through the same struggles. One very practical book along those lines is *Living with your Husband's Secret Wars* by Marsha Means. Another good book, one written by a wife of a former sex addict, is *Through Deep Waters: Letters to Hurting Wives* by Kathy Gallagher. In addition, read this book and other books your husband reads as he strives for purity so that you'll grow with him (but not so you can point out his shortcomings).

Become a part of his healing process. Don't just focus on areas where he fails to live up to your expectations. But, please remember to encourage him when he succeeds. Be interested and active, but in a loving and gentle way. In addition, be patient during this process. It will take some time for the pain to subside and for full trust to be rebuilt. For instance, try not to be overly suspicious when your husband comes home a few minutes late.

Get together with other women; you're not alone, so don't isolate. If your husband balks at you telling others, ask him to read this book, including this chapter. At the same time, remember this is a matter of great shame to your husband. Be respectful and loving toward him and in your conversations with others. Generally, you should avoid telling your parents about it (at least not the full extent of his sins) because they may not welcome or forgive him, even long after you forgive your husband and are doing better.

If you feel the need, it's okay to ask your husband to attend marriage counseling. It's important that you both are moving forward together and sometimes a coach can be helpful in the process.

Focus on your own Spiritual Growth

It's important that you use this time as an opportunity for reflection and spiritual growth. Ask the Lord what He is trying to teach you. Even if you feel like you are a victim to your husband's issues, you have issues too.

Begin by focusing on your own shortcomings and sins. For instance, have you been angry, bossy, bitter, or nit picky? These things affect you and your husband spiritually. They should be acknowledged and confessed as sin. The natural tendency is to focus on the sins of your husband, i.e., if he were not selfish I would not have to complain. Make it your goal to restore your relationship with both Jesus and your husband, and don't let anger, bitterness or anything else stand in the way.

Always keep going to Jesus seeking His mercy, grace and strength to carry on. Get involved in a Bible believing church where you are loved unconditionally. Attend a women's Bible study if it is available. Constantly strive for a closer relationship with Jesus Christ. In fact, make it your number one priority.

Two Tough Topics

Now here are two difficult recommendations. First, don't withhold sex. Part of your husband's sex addiction involves a conditioning of his mind and body to need sex. It will make the process harder for him if he has to fight the physical withdrawal together with shame and other consequences of his sinful behaviors.

(Of course, if your husband has had an affair, you don't need to have any type of sexual contact that would put you at risk of a disease. Wait until after he gets tested.)

Second, don't threaten to leave. You may be tempted to tell your husband that if he looks at pornography one more time you will file for divorce. All this does is tell your husband that it is better for him to keep secrets and that you aren't willing to hear the truth or work through difficulties. Wouldn't you rather be a safe woman for your husband and value honesty? You've already discovered what secrets can do to you personally. God is honest with us no matter how painful the truth can be. The truth can be dealt with. But lies never allow for healing and restoration.

It's better to know the difficult truth that your husband has trained his mind to lust and is in need of help in correcting his backward thinking. It won't just happen overnight and he will occasionally slip back into old ways. If you allow him to be open and honest with you about the struggle—including any setbacks or miscues—you will be able to work openly with him in moving forward down the healing path. This also helps build trust. The alternative is to have him believe the lie of Satan that it is better to keep a secret life from you and only tell you of victories. Therefore, plan on staying the course. Give the Lord time to usher in healing and change.

I am not saying that there is never a time or good reason for separation. Before you do, be sure to get guidance from your pastor and Godly women. In addition, don't expect that he will never have a setback. This process takes time. A life of repentance is the key, not a life of perfection. Fight to keep an eternal perspective. For instance, focus upon the hope of a restored marriage, even knowing that it will require much effort, and fight against the desire to give up that occurs when you focus on how difficult and painful the process is.

Additional Remarks

Be mindful of avoiding things that may undermine his recovery. For instance, don't schedule events on nights he has a support group meeting. You can also assist in his recovery in many ways, such as monitoring together what TV shows you watch. Most shows contain sexually suggestive content. If he wants to give up TV for a season, be willing to sacrifice and play games or engage in other activities. Similarly, be aware of what magazines you leave around the house.

One more suggestion. If either you or your husband have had sexual abuse issues, I urge you to read together one of the following books: *Rid of My Disgrace* by Justin and Lindsey Holcomb (Crossway) or *The Wounded Heart* by Dr. Dan Allender (NavPress). If these issues are a hindrance to your marriage, I also urge you to seek Christian counseling.

And finally, I want to remind you that you are not alone. There is hope. My marriage is better today than when we first got married. It was hard to forgive and trust my husband again, but it was worth every tear and all of the effort. Besides, the Lord promises to use all our pain and struggles for His glory. Just as we hope our husbands will become needy, dependent servants of the Lord, we too must turn to and trust in the Lord during our darkest moments and strive to live out the same six elements of a Proven life necessary for a healthy marriage. Be patient and an active participant of the process. Keep praying for your husband and looking for ways to build him up.

A Note for Single Women

Because single women have not made wedding vows, which have longer lasting repercussions to their lives, they have a different decision to make. What they need to wrestle with is whether they can deal with this particular life challenge. They still need to bear in mind that all men (and all women) will have some major issue in life. The question is whether they can live with this particular stronghold. It's better to know prior to marriage whether you can view this as a "we problem" and not a "he problem."

My Perspective as A Husband and Group Leader

As a group leader for many years, I am constantly aware that everyone has one issue in their life that they cannot win on their own. I believe God does this for our own good so that we don't try to live independently from Him. For some wives, it is also sexual sins, and for others it may be worry or gossip. Don't get me wrong. I am not saying that all forms of sin are as painful as betrayal in the form of sexual sin. But my point is that humans are prone to sin and setbacks.

When I first began leading purity support groups ten years ago, I wished that every man in my groups would immediately stop looking at pornography or masturbating. But it didn't work out that way. In fact, even many of the small group leaders that I handpicked and trained after they went through the *12-week Study* had at least one setback while leading a group. I spent a lot of time trying to figure out if I was a poor trainer or if my *Study* was not effective. What I have concluded is that none of us will remain sinless, but we can daily strive to be Proven Men. I am convinced that the Lord is very pleased by our striving to turn to and rely on Him even though it includes setbacks. God loves a needy, dependent servant who sometimes has a setback; just read the life of David in the Bible.

I love leading weekly support groups. What excites me most is seeing spiritual growth. I am constantly amazed as I hear story-after-story of men share what they have learned and how they have grown spiritually after a setback. I certainly don't glorify setbacks, but I have tears of joy whenever I listen to a man describe the way he has experienced the Lord in new or deeper ways after he has repented and experienced forgiveness. I love listening to them share what they have learned from the Lord. Perhaps I view it as the harder the struggle, the sweeter the victory.

Men grow closer to the Lord through these trials than they do when they have had an easy week. I imagine that it brings God more glory for those hopeless and helpless without Him who scrap and scrape through toil each moment of each day to fight for purity but have some setbacks along the way, than for God to simply take away every lustful thought or deed. I love watching men grow in the Lord over 12 weeks of the support group. I constantly remind men that the 12 weeks is just the beginning of the process. This is just a time of learning the basic fundamentals, and that it will take a lifetime of effort to keep growing in their faith and the sanctification process on earth.

I privately tell men that I am glad that I had a sin I couldn't defeat on my own. What I really mean is that I am glad that God didn't just take away the sin. I am glad that it was the hardest battle of my life. I am glad I couldn't just give it up with one prayer or one meeting with another man. If God had simply taken it away, I would not have learned to rely on Him. I would never have gotten to know God as a daily Lord and Savior. I would have kept relying on myself. I would never have learned to hug another man. I would never have experienced the freedom to raise my hands in praise to God. I would never have wanted to talk about my feelings or see the need to be open and honest in discussions with my wife. I would never have known a real marriage. In the end, I would be the same proud and selfish man, without one particular sin I found disgusting.

The reality is that most men going through Proven Men support groups stumble. I don't use shame or guilt to try to get them to step in line because that is not how Jesus works. He uses unconditional love to draw us to Him. Thus, I have learned to tell men that victory is not absence of sin, but how they respond to it. Let me repeat that. The mark of a Proven Man is not whether he sins, but how he responds to a setback. In fact, a setback is an opportunity to learn from and lean upon God. I would rather have a man who repents than one who pretends he is setback free, and I am sure you do too.

As a former sex addict who sinned and deeply wounded his wife, but now leads support groups, I encourage all the wives reading this chapter to emulate Christ, who values openness, offers unconditional love, and is committed to being a helper.

Encourage your man to keep striving to be a Proven Man, knowing there is no perfect husband or wife. Both sexual healing and marriage are lifelong commitments. Be patient, courageous, and willing to join your husband as a partner fighting against the spiritual forces at work to defeat your husband and your marriage.

Passionate for God,
Repentant in spirit,
Open and honest,
Victorious in living,
Eternal in perspective, and
Networking with other *Proven Men.*

Full Stories of Joel, Tim and Stan

JOEL
The Overachiever with Only One Thing He Couldn't Overcome

I was a typical overachiever. My parents told me I could do or be anything I wanted and I believed it. Everything I put my mind to, I accomplished. In grade school, I was the teacher's pet and regularly praised for early accomplishments. As captain of the track team, I added acclaim in sports to good grades in high school. College and law school exams presented no obstacle; I graduated in the top 5 in my law school class. In one summer, I aced the Bar exam, married the homecoming queen, and landed a prestigious job. I regularly received bonuses and awards for accomplishments.

Yet there is one thing I couldn't overcome. I was addicted to lust and masturbation. There was much more going on than my looking at porn or lusting after women. There was an ever-present inner tension between my duality, as I desperately sought to compartmentalize my competing secret life from my public one. It was hard to bring my two worlds together. On the outside, I had a clean cup; on the inside, filth. To compensate, I made my outside appearance the cleanest in the land. Yet, guilt and shame never vanished. At times it was overwhelming. Will my secret life prevail or will my entire world crash around me?

A Secret Life

Before I became a Proven Man, almost daily I waited every night for my wife to go to sleep; then I would begin mentally downloading all the pictures I purposed to capture in my mind throughout the day. My heart would race as I scrolled through images. Who would it be tonight? I would spend nearly an hour every night conjuring up fantasies based on the women I saw that day. I might pretend the blonde invites me to her apartment or the redhead wants sex in the back seat of her car. I would come up with dozens of scenarios based on the top picks of the day, culminating in masturbation.

On other occasions, I would see one of the model's eyes while having sex with my wife. Either way, by morning guilt and shame would nip at my heels. I hated that part of this life—the guilt and shame. I tried countless times to stop masturbating. But defeating the monster of lust and its tentacle of masturbation or pornography was the one thing that eluded me in life.

If I had measured the number of invented fantasies that played in my mind while masturbating, the number would easily have reached 250,000, based on 35 lustful thoughts a day for 20 years. I had given myself over to sexual fantasy; it transcended my everyday life. I sexualized almost everything. Nearly every pretty woman I met, I undressed with my eyes or saved her image for later use.

The World Closing in on Me

On the other hand, I was one of the nicest young men you could ever meet. I reminded myself that I didn't lie, cheat, steal, smoke, drink, or swear. And I could count on one hand the number of times I missed church. During law school, at age 27, I had accepted Jesus as Savior and had soon met a woman I fell in love with. We were married within a year. Everything was falling into place. However, the lustful thoughts and masturbation didn't go away. As I became a married Christian man, I still maintained my former fantasy life. In fact, I continued to keep opening my mind daily to sensuality. I was fixated on beautiful women in TV shows, commercials, or magazines. Even on the way to work I "noticed" (and captured their image in my mind) sensually dressed women. My constant lustful thoughts only heightened my desire more for sex, making me think I needed it every day.

Before long, my wife and I were involved in many activities at church and were viewed as a model couple. I knew I needed help, but was too proud and ashamed to ask. Yet my world seemed to be closing in on me and I needed to find a way of escape. I knew that it was just a matter of time before I would have an affair and drive my wife away—and she was too precious to lose. No matter how many times I promised myself that I would abstain, after about three weeks I would begin masturbating again. In fact, my thoughts and actions continued to grow more and more impure.

Escape from Temptation

When did it all start? When I was twelve, I found a *Playboy* magazine hidden under a bed. As I looked at the pictures of the naked women, I began fantasizing about sex. In fact, I soon became fixated on sex. I began seeing women as objects of desire. I developed a lifestyle of masturbating almost daily while thinking about sexual images or fantasies. Although I felt guilty afterward, each night as I closed my eyes sexual thoughts flooded my mind and I would begin the ritual all over again.

In high school I actually went to an X-rated movie and even to a topless bar. At 18, I bought a few *Playboy* magazines, as well as some hard-core pornography. But more than those things, my issue was that sex was always on my mind. I didn't need the stimulus of pornography because I could easily find sexual images or ideas almost everywhere. It was my mind that was polluted. I purposefully stored images in my mind of faces or bodies of women I met during the day to use for masturbation at night.

During college I began having sex. This only fueled the fire more. I continued to fantasize and masturbate. Each relationship ultimately ended without satisfaction. Although deep down I knew lustful thoughts and masturbation were wrong, I held on to the belief that, as soon as I got married, it would stop. It didn't. Even seven years into my marriage, I was regularly lusting and masturbating.

After I married, I knew I needed to stop dreaming of sex with other women. Naturally, I first relied upon my own efforts. I took cold showers and even sought sex with my wife daily. But the intense desire for "just a little bit more" was never quenched. Repeatedly, I vowed to put an end to masturbation. Yet, it merely ushered in fresh rounds of failure, guilt and shame, as vow after vow was broken. Nothing had worked because none of my actions addressed the root issues giving rise to the sensual desire, and none of my efforts relied on the strength of the Lord.

Although I believed my intentions to be good, at the core, my motive for asking God to remove the temptation was not pure. I didn't want to replace false intimacy with real and open relationships. I still wanted love without the pain associated with real relationships. I believed sex to be my own unmet need and equated sex with love. This lie kept me in bondage to sexual sin for many years. I was growing tired of my secret life of a double agent and constant failure. It wasn't until I was close to having a physical affair that I conceded I would never be able to climb my way to freedom on my own. I was finally willing to ask for help.

Admitting the Problem

In the end, I became so afraid of acting out on one of my thousands of sexual fantasies and actually committing adultery that I went to the pastor of my church and admitted that I had a sex problem that I couldn't overcome. The pastor didn't reject me, but cried with me and hugged me. He reassured me and told me that he loved me. I couldn't believe the pastor didn't judge me or throw me out of church. It marked a new direction for me. I felt a great weight had been lifted. I even dared to harbor the thought, "If the pastor didn't reject me, maybe my wife or God won't either." I went home and confessed to my wife all of my sins—my sexual fantasies, selfishness and my pride—and went through 12 weeks of Biblical counseling for sexual integrity. After that, I was finally willing to surrender this one last area of my life to God.

Willing to do whatever it took, I began meeting weekly with a man who had overcome sexual addiction himself. He reassured me that it was possible to live in freedom. I knew there was much work ahead, but I also knew there was hope. I was 100 percent committed to being changed by God and willing to do whatever it took to live a pure life in dependency upon Him.

The more I surrendered to God and began allowing Christ to live through me, the more the Lord carried me to purity and a place of rest. The Proven Path opened an entire new and rich manner of knowing God and provided tools for seeking after the Lord with all of my heart. But don't misunderstand. It was a lot of work and I was in for the fight of my life.

Letting Go of Pride

Early on in the process, my wife was not so sure that I would change. After all, I had been unfaithful to her in my heart from Day One of our marriage. I still remember clearly something she told me that helped change the course of my life: "You are just sorry about the consequences, but you don't really see your conduct as wrong." I had wanted to disagree, but deep inside knew she was absolutely right. I hated the consequences, but didn't really want to stop. I had not seen lustful thoughts or masturbation as something that grieved God or as something evil. I had enjoyed the false intimacy of fantasy, lust and masturbation, but I had finally reached the point where I knew I needed to die to lust and live for the Lord.

By God's mercy, my wife didn't abandon me. She stood by my side every step of the way. Of course, it took a long time to regain her trust. But for the first time I truly was willing to do whatever it took to stop sinning and start living for purposes greater than my own selfishness. I received Biblical counseling weekly from another Christian man who had been set free from addiction to sex. He started by being open about not being perfect. The safe environment gave me the opportunity to be real—to be myself.

I began to see that my thinking was backward. I saw that my selfishness and pride had fueled my lust. I finally realized that the only hope I had was in turning over all areas of my life to Jesus. I needed to adopt God's plan for living instead of my own. Daily, I spent much time in Bible study and prayer. I began to understand the root sin issues beneath the sexual behavior. I confessed my struggles to a trusted friend, who helped hold me accountable.

I really wanted to be totally free from the bondage of lust and sexual impurity. But more than that, I wanted to return home to God, to live out of love, and to live for Jesus. It was then that I finally began living a victorious life free from the grip of lust and masturbation.

During this process, I began seeing how selfish I had been. I had loved the praise of others. I even thought that somehow God loved me more than the others. I finally understood that I was proud and my pride was fighting against the Lord. It was no wonder I was stuck in bondage to masturbation; I was selfish in everything I did. God needed to break my pride before I could truly be free of sexual sin and all the other sins driven by my selfishness.

Planning for Triggers

I had trained myself to sexualize everything. For instance, I positioned myself to be at the right place to look down a woman's blouse, especially if she may need to bend over. Every time I entered a room, I would know where every woman was and had ranked them in order of beauty. I barely met a pretty woman I didn't include in my fantasies, even some of my friends' wives. In fact, my sinful motto was "staring, glaring, and comparing." There were so many bad behaviors leading to bad inputs that it would take an all-out battle to have victory.

I was determined to change and be stamped PROVEN. I would eliminate the bad inputs. For instance, I stared at the ground on my subway commute. I would even stand to the right side and close my left eye when riding up escalators so I would not look at the women walking up the escalator past me. I even gave up watching TV for a year because I tended to lust after women in shows or commercials.

But that wasn't enough. I needed a plan for the triggers, such as when I had a fight with my wife. When we fought, I had often thought to myself, who needs her. I would escape into fantasy through masturbation. I also knew that the shopping mall was a bad place, so I didn't go there for months. I went through the effort of thinking through every trigger and put into place a game plan for each. That's because if I was not prepared for each different setting I knew I would react the way I had trained myself to lust.

An example of a game plan for traveling out of town on business included letting my networking partner know. When I got into the hotel room, I would unplug the TV and place a towel over the screen. That way I needed two steps to turn it on. Also, I brought my Bible study to do and an encouraging book to read at night to *replace* TV. I would also call my wife each evening.

Done Pretending

Initially, I was only pretending that I wanted to stop lust and masturbation. I had given Christ every part of my heart, well all except this one small, tiny little place. It was so small that it would not show up on an X-ray machine. I had convinced myself that God would overlook it when compared to how much else I did for God. The times when I cried out to the Lord to take away the temptation, I was really only interested in ridding myself of guilt. I thought I couldn't live without the nightly escape into fantasy.

It wasn't until my marriage was on the line that I had to make a choice between the real woman God provided to me and the fake ones I created. I had to answer the question, "Do I want to get well?" Now, for the first time, I really could say yes. I was finally willing to go through life relying on the Lord instead of the temporary relief of masturbation. I was determined to have conviction, faith, and action. No more games. No more secret lives.

The shovel analogy also really struck home. I was the classic man who believed, "I can do it myself." In fact, my dad had raised me to live by the motto: "If I can't do it myself, I don't need it." My father taught me that it was a sign of weakness to ask anyone for help.

Finally, I understood why the Lord had allowed one thing to remain in my life that was too big for me. If I didn't have to rely upon the Lord for purity, I would have been puffed up with pride claiming I beat it on my own. I would have kept living my life on my own for my own. But that's not God's way. The Lord opposes the proud, but gives grace to the humble. I finally chose to humble myself and stop fighting against God.

Although frightened to be out of control, I was going to put down the shovel of self-effort and become a servant of God. I would turn to the Lord for strength and rely on God. That meant rising each day to meet with God and start listening to His voice. I would ask the Lord to be the pilot to purity. I would start doing things God's way.

Swinging the Sword with a Soft Heart

The process wasn't easy. I was a man of action. I wanted to fight temptation and defeat the enemy of lust. Therefore, it was hard for me to hear that I needed to put down the shovel of self-effort. I agreed.

As soon as I humbled myself before the Lord, it was exciting to learn that God did want me to participate in the battle. The Lord had a sword for me to use. I was also given other armor to wear during the battle. This time, however, I would follow God. I would begin meeting with the Lord each morning, not to check off homework, but to get to know Him. I wanted a soft heart, to be humble, to follow God's way.

Part of picking up the sword was to recognize that lust and pornography are evil, and attack them as a doctor attacks cancer. I would eradicate the worldly influences and build my life around Godly pursuits. I didn't just want to leave a vacant house behind, but to fill it with the Lord. I gradually became fully committed to sexual integrity. I was going to fight using God's weapons, including memorizing weekly verses. I would stand firm, and rely on the Lord through every temptation.

Learning to Ruin the Moment

Because I had spent 20 years sexualizing everything, the temptations to lust kept knocking at my door every moment of every day. Each morning I had to make a new commitment to purity. For the first few weeks, it seemed as if I was confessing sexual thoughts every minute of my subway commute, but I was determined. So I developed a game plan for my commute. I brought a Bible study with me to read while seated and look only at the ground while walking, since each time I had looked above a woman's ankles, I was tempted to think about her in a sexual way.

I was determined to recognize each and every impure thought. For instance, if a woman sat in the seat next to me, and if I glanced at her and noticed her bust, I would close my eyes or look away to ruin the moment immediately. I would acknowledge and confess the thought as sinful and ask God for forgiveness. I would then immediately replace the thought by reading a Bible verse.

It was not easy. It felt like I was in a fox hole during a war. I might easily confess ten times to lustful thoughts during my 45 minute commute to work. Each time I would keep repeating, "not an option, not an option," in order to ruin the moment. I couldn't let the thought linger or it would fuel my old nature where I ultimately would replay the thought while masturbating. But now, it was no longer an option. Yet, at times, the image of a woman kept appearing in my mind, so I would repeat to myself: "I refuse to take pleasure." I did this each time a tempting thought tried entering my mind. It often took a few times of repeating this for the image to fade away. At times, that was not even enough and I had to rapidly blink my eyes to erase the image. I would also replace the thought with something pure, such as the wonderful wife God had provided or a verse of Scripture spelling out one of the promises of God.

In the early days, I would have an internal discussion that went something like this: "Lust is a sin. God hates sin. Therefore, I hate to lust." Sometimes I had to repeat it three times to drown out the small voice that murmured in the back of my head, "What's the big deal? No one is hurt."

But I trusted God and wanted to retrain my backward thinking. Therefore, I reminded myself all day every day that lust, pornography, and masturbation were all unwelcome in my life.

After a few weeks, I knew that I had to stop watching television because I lusted after the actresses. Even watching football was not safe due to the commercials. I had such a resolve for holiness that I eventually gave up all movies and TV for an entire year.

Initially, my wife was upset because that meant we couldn't watch TV together. At first, we just sat on the couch, looking at each other and wondering what we would do to replace our TV time. But when we began playing board games together, we started to get to know each other for the first time. We began talking and sharing. To our surprise, giving up TV was the best thing that had happened to us.

I was no longer content to wait until the end of the day or week to recount and confess the sexual sinful thoughts and repent. I repented on the spot, even as I pushed a sexual thought from my mind. This was one of the keys that kept me from returning to the lifelong habit of masturbating each day. I realized that if I ruined every sexual thought in my mind, it would be impossible to masturbate again.

Filling an Empty Room

I had not really wanted to be well for 20 years. I merely wanted the struggle to go away. I hated the guilt and shame, but secretly loved the pleasurable parts of fantasy and masturbation. Deep inside I knew that I didn't want to give God control of the part of my life that would keep fantasy as an escape option. I felt I needed that crutch.

When I finally made masturbation and my connected fantasy world no longer an option, I was scared because that was my treasured secret escape. Not wanting to ever return back to that double-agent life, I became desperate for Christ to fill the empty room and to give me strength. I trusted the Lord by giving Him my whole heart, this time every square inch. I gave God access to and control over my thought life. I truly wanted to get well. I took on Galatians 2:20 as my life verse to combat self-pride; I died to self and agreed to live in and through the Lord. I was done trusting in my abilities. I was putting God in charge of all areas of my life.

It would be the hardest battle of my life, but it was also the sweetest one. Part of doing whatever it takes was relying daily upon the Lord for strength. From a proud self-doer, I became a needy, dependent servant of Christ. I began experiencing true and daily intimacy with the Lord for the first time. I also no longer had secrets to keep. I felt free. As a result, my relationship with my wife began to flourish. It was even better in all areas than when we first married!

From Addict to Elder

Fifteen years ago was the last time I looked at pornography or masturbated. Three years after I first truly gave up my secret and shameful ways, I began burning with passion to help other men break free, so I formed my first sexual integrity support group and began writing a study to help others. A year later, the IRS granted me non-profit status for Proven Men Ministries, and I began taking this ministry around the world.

Leading up to that time, my life was being radically transformed. Everyone began noticing a change in me. I was not the same person who argued all the time and had to be right or win at everything. My wife's friends would secretly ask her what happened, hoping there was some formula that they could give to their husbands. Even my church leaders saw a new and Proven Man in me and I am now an elder at my local church.

My stamp of PROVEN was not awarded because of a certain number of days I have not masturbated, but remains based upon a heart that purposes to put into practice each of the six letters of the acronym.

Won't you join me? Be on Guard. Live a Proven life.

TIM
The Underachiever Who Shied Away
from Real Relationships

"You're so stupid. I don't think you have the brains you were born with!" These were hard words. It was especially devastating because they came from his father, a man he looked up to. Harsh words and disappointment were the norm in Tim's life. His father made a point of telling him, "You're no good. You'll never amount to anything." Tim tried to dismiss his father, but in his heart he couldn't help but believe these assessments of himself. Actually, the inability to please his father shattered Tim's very soul. It produced intense shame, guilt and self-condemnation. "I must be defective. I don't deserve his love. I don't deserve anyone's love," Tim told himself.

Add to this the extreme guilt and shame over masturbation and you have a train wreck waiting to happen. As a child, Tim once stumbled upon a box of pornography in his uncle's work shed. It was like manna from heaven, providing a way of experiencing the human love and respect that he so desperately longed to enjoy. Will he be able to give up this one consolation and turn to God?

Hiding in the Closet

Long before he had the vision to see that God could provide the victory in his life, Tim struggled in constant bondage to the idea that he had to prove himself with his efforts alone. His whole world revolved around his performance: "Am I good enough? Can I measure up to the standard?" If Tim failed to be perfect in anything, he was the first to beat himself up. He lived in constant stress, wondering when he would fail next. In his mind he treated himself as his father would have, assuming that his efforts were still not up to par because he probably could have done it better or faster.

His only escape was pornography. All Tim needed to do was flip through the pages and select one of many willing lovers. This fantasy world allowed Tim to escape reality. It would be the safe place where he would never have to hear that he was no good or disappoint anyone. The pleasure of masturbation confirmed that this was the world to remain hidden in. It was far safer living in a fantasy world than risking further rejection. Tim turned to masturbation in place of open relationships. He would sneak magazines to his bedroom closet so he would never be alone again.

As with all sin, its pleasures were temporary. Tim's self-condemnation for escaping into his closet robbed him of real pleasure in life. Any measure of appreciation from a real person was met with skepticism. Internally, Tim knew better. He was not worthy. Tim's biggest fear was that he would be eventually found out. Like so many others addicted to sex, Tim was plagued with the assumption that "if others really knew me, they would not like me." Tim reasoned that if his father had hated what he saw in Tim, everyone else must hate his imperfections, too. He couldn't trust his feelings or share his thoughts with anyone. It would be best not to allow anyone inside. Therefore, Tim made a vow to never tell another human soul that he masturbated.

A Sinking Ship

Tim's assumption that he was no good made him vow never to date when he was in the Christian boarding school where his father sent him. Even though Tim heard the words of the Gospel of love and peace at school, he assumed it was for others, not him. It never broke the barriers of his closed heart.

As an adult, the constant strain of failing to meet his dad's expectations was met with a bottle of booze at night and frequent trips to the bathroom during the day to lose himself in pornography and masturbation. Tim would work twelve hours, then go straight to the bar. Soon Tim began going to strip clubs. For $120 per hour, a real woman would sit next to Tim and talk. They never had sex or even talked of sex, but it was the closest thing to intimacy Tim ever had.

Condemnation

At his lowest emotional point, Tim's weight rose to 300 pounds. He had no expectations of ever dating a girl or pleasing his dad. Tim couldn't risk another rejection. He would retreat into fantasy, porn and masturbate himself to sleep every night.

Tim knew the basic Bible verses from Sunday school. But his idea of being crucified with Christ meant to debase himself with condemning thoughts. Throughout his life, his dad kept telling him he would never amount to anything. Tim knew he could never measure up, so he frequently stopped trying. Adding more burden to his soul was Tim's view that taking up the cross of Christ meant carrying the load himself. He was always burdened and defeat was his constant companion.

Tim eventually did get married to the first girl he dated—a woman from work who asked him out, but he hid from her his feelings, hopes and dreams. Tim was constantly pretending to be someone else and never let his guard down. The drinking and masturbation continued in full force. Tim felt certain that he didn't deserve a wife so beautiful and caring. He had no idea what she saw in him. Since Tim couldn't afford to risk losing her, it was simple: "I must never let her see the real me."

They attended church each week and she became quite active in women's ministries. Tim pretended to be spiritual and learned the Christian talk. However, whenever she left for a meeting, Tim would shout, "I am free!" That meant drinking and watching pornography. What happened next was every man's worst nightmare. Tim's wife came home early one night to find a XXX-rated DVD on the coffee table. His wife looked at him with tears flowing from her eyes as she held the DVD and asked him "Why?" He knew why, but he couldn't tell her. He couldn't let her inside. He couldn't reveal his fears.

Tim was at a crossroads. His wife was going to leave if he didn't attend Proven Men. The choice was hard, but Tim thought he could fake another phase of his life. He was a master at it. Tim would attend in person, but continue to conceal his heart. He could never admit his failure. He would be destroyed if anyone learned that he was so messed up that he had to masturbate up to 10 times a day just to cope with reality.

Pride, Posing as Low Self-Esteem

Tim made sure he came to each Proven Men meeting. In fact, Tim's wife had it marked on the calendar so he couldn't "forget." At first, the 12-week *Study* was more than Tim could handle. Of course that was partly because each night Tim was still watching TV at 2:00 a.m. to escape reality, leaving him no time to complete the exercises in the *Study*.

But there was something about attending the weekly group meetings that allured him. It was the first place he could tell someone he was a mess and not get beaten up. No matter how much he shared, he was not judged. His heart was beginning to soften. He frequently cried during the group as new feelings kept surfacing. Tim now actually longed to be made well.

Tim generally understood how pride was a main root that fueled sexual sins. But was he also filled with pride? Initially he couldn't believe it. How could a person with such a low self-esteem be proud? As he reflected more, he could see how his self-condemnation was actually another manifestation of pride. Because Tim couldn't stand not being perfect, he often didn't even try.

For instance, because he didn't think his advertisements were perfect, he didn't send any out to attract new customers. Each time he didn't measure up to perfection, he beat himself up. Even in the area of sex, his pride had been the root problem. He started to see that because he didn't get what he "deserved," he indulged himself in masturbation. He also saw how his escape into fantasy was based in pride, posing as low self-esteem, like a wolf in sheep's clothing.

It was the fear of not being seen as perfect that caused Tim to hide in fantasy and false intimacy. Dealing with his pride would be hard and it would take time to undo his self-condemnation, but Proven Men gave him the right start and the Lord will finish the work in him.

Finding Acceptance

Tim was only willing to start attending the purity group because he was afraid his wife would leave. Although he had little choice but to attend the next Proven Men session, Tim knew he needed to find out what he was getting into so he could protect himself. He carefully watched the leader of the group at other church functions. He noticed his every move, his every word to others, so he could understand what kind of a man this was. "Would he be holier-than-thou? Would he be puffed up? Would he be judgmental?" At least from a distance, the man seemed real, open and approachable. Most importantly, he didn't seem to use harsh words. Others seemed to respect him. Maybe it would not be so bad.

Just to be safe, Tim decided to test the leader by only giving him a few details of his secret sin to see how the man would react. When the leader showed him unconditional love, Tim was shocked. At first, he wasn't sure how to take it. His own father had never treated him with such simple, yet complete, acceptance. Tim began to wonder whether the promises in the Bible just might hold true for him. Tim saw the heart of God through the heart of a man and it gave him hope. Maybe, just maybe, he could change his ways. With his marriage on the line, he had no real choice but to risk it all and open his heart to the Lord.

In the months that followed, Tim found that, no matter what secrets he revealed to the leader, he was always met with acceptance and grace. If a man could respond in this way, surely God would be even more accepting.

Another thing Tim didn't expect was that the man leading Proven Men seemed to see right through him and yet he refused to judge or push him away. Instead, he hugged him and told him that he loved him. With such deep, open-hearted acceptance, it was not long before Tim told the man his whole story. A part of him hoped the leader would reject him and run away, as Tim expected. It would have proved he had been right all along. But another, stronger part of him yearned to believe that God's healing was really attainable for him. This man was Tim's litmus test. For the first time, Tim began to believe that God the Father was really a loving Father—a Father he could open his heart to.

Doing Business with Triggers

Tim had many triggers, such as being lonely or bored. The biggest was any time someone said something critical. It brought him back to when his dad told him he was worthless. Tim's reaction would be to hide in fantasy and masturbation.

During one Proven Men meeting, Tim mentioned that when someone says, "Hey, Tim," the hairs on his neck stand up and he recoils with fear. His dad had always started with that phrase when criticizing him. To inspire Tim, the Proven Men leader wrote a song that week and sang it to Tim at the next meeting. It was named "Hey, Tim," and each refrain was similar to this: "Hey, Tim, don't you know that I love you; Hey, Tim, I think you are the greatest." Although the music was off tune, it was sweet music for Tim, who wept like a child.

Over time, Tim began believing that the Lord loves him and that God is worthy to be served. Therefore Tim started doing business with his triggers. For instance, he stopped going out to lunch to avoid places where he ate desserts as a prelude and used the restrooms to carry out his action. Now, his plan included talking to his wife about his painful past and his fear of intimacy. In addition, Tim carried with him on a note card his life verse of Romans 8:1 *(Therefore, there is no condemnation for those in Christ Jesus)*. He would also purpose to reject instead of dwelling on the condemning thoughts that wanted to flood his mind. He would also replace ugly thoughts by looking at a picture of his wife and child and praise the Lord for them.

Tim began taking on new challenges, willing to risk not being perfect. To his amazement, he could lead. He no longer worked for his dad, but bought his own shop. He also took risks by leading at home. His wife was grateful that she didn't have to carry the load by herself anymore.

Self-Effort: Who Me?

In his own mind, Tim couldn't do anything right, so it was not hard for him to believe that he needed to put down the shovel of self-effort. But actually Tim was holding just as tight a grip on the shovel as Joel. Tim was committed to control. He desperately needed to control his relationships in order to control the pain. Tim had learned not to trust anyone. He carefully chose what entered his life. He rarely tried anything new and relied on no one, not even God. In fact, Tim was fearful that if he gave God control, the Lord would send him to India to be a missionary. Tim was definitely afraid to give God control.

If Tim couldn't learn to trust God, he couldn't stop striving in his own strength. Because the Lord wanted to bring healing to Tim, he sent a man into his life who would not judge; someone to show unconditional love. The outpouring of grace through a man caused Tim to see God as a loving father for the first time. It gave Tim hope. Tim now realized he could trust the Lord. The more Tim trusted God, the more his heart melted. He began having feelings. He began being open and honest.

Picking up the Sword

In a choice between fight or flight, Tim inevitably chooses flight. He always ran away from confrontation. During high school Tim was the largest kid in school, wearing size 14 shoes that supported his 300 pounds. The football coach made Tim join the team. The problem was that Tim didn't want to hit anyone with his pads. The coach tried to change that through a special session where the coach's kid, who was 150 pounds lighter, was told to keep running at Tim to try to knock him out. Tim easily shoved him away with his hands on every try. When the coach began berating his son for being weak, it was Tim who ran off crying. Tim never put on the pads again.

Tim's fear of confrontation and rejection also affected his marriage. He refused to lead his wife at home or make any decisions, even which restaurant to go to or where to park the car. He didn't want to make yet another mistake. Therefore he didn't have any practice engaging in a battle. It would take everything in him to be willing to stand beside the Lord and fight for purity. Fortunately, his Proven Men leader was patient. He spent time getting to know and encourage Tim. For instance, he suggested that Tim take on Romans 8:1 as his life verse: "Therefore, there is now no condemnation for those who are in Christ Jesus." Tim grew to trust in God's power and to believe He is good. He was now willing to pick up the sword God had for him.

Giving up Consolation

Tim's only safe world had been fantasy, porn and masturbation, so it was especially hard for Tim to agree to stop fantasizing. But Tim had formed a pattern of finding the nearest fast food chain to indulge in a dessert, then using the restroom to masturbate. This was the reason he was both overweight and addicted to masturbation.

Sexual purity was a much taller order for Tim than it is for many men. Tim would make it a few days using his own willpower, but if his dad humiliated him and made him feel worthless, it was often more than Tim could handle. He would take consolation in sexual release.

Once he had joined the group, Tim lied in the beginning, saying that he had not masturbated during the week, but his guilt overwhelmed him. He called the leader and confessed by telephone. The leader told Tim that he loved him and understood his battle. He prayed with Tim and gave him encouragement—without guilt, shame or judgment. Tim gradually realized that the group was really safe and began to confess his setbacks, as well as his victories. As the weeks progressed, Tim had more periods of victory than defeat.

For Tim a 12-week study was too short. Tim begged the leader to let him start again in the next study. Of course, the leader agreed. Tim stopped masturbating weekly. He embraced the belief that

God was good and would not discard him. Tim fought hard to use the three Rs, always having a life verse handy reminding him that God didn't condemn him (as his own father had). Tim knew he was forgiven each time and began wanting to please the Lord through purity. God was meeting with Tim. He felt that God did love him after all. Tim was finally willing to do whatever it takes—God's way this time.

Giving Up His Life

After going through the Proven Men purity study twice, Tim stopped looking at porn or daily masturbating (although still stumbling on a few occasions). Even though Tim was head and shoulders above where he began, he was not experiencing the fullness of intimacy with his wife, both emotionally and sexually. He and his wife started attending marriage counseling, but couldn't put their finger on the problem. Finally, his Proven Men small group leader suggested that there was something Tim was still holding back in his relationship, the same reason why he occasionally returned to masturbation. The leader asked Tim to make an irrevocable decision that *masturbation was no longer an option,* such that he would give up anything that contributed to his fall. That meant nothing could be off limits, even refusing to travel for his job. This jolted Tim. Up until then, Tim thought that he had given up masturbation. Now he realized that he had been unwilling to risk everything to remain pure. He knew he had never really committed in his heart that it was never an option.

That day Tim fell before God and put his entire life and his job on the altar. No matter what the cost, masturbation was no longer an option, period. Almost immediately, Tim's intimacy with his wife began to flourish. Something inside him just clicked when he made this covenant. It was now just he and his wife. Thus, if he had a fight with his wife, he couldn't slip away into fantasy. He had to deal with her and real life without any escapes. This ushered in change and dependency on the Lord!

Tim also began taking risks opening up to his wife in new and intimate ways. It was remarkable how his wife was responding. She commented that it was like they were having the honeymoon they never had. His wife was so excited about the change that she used the *Proven Men Study* as her next Bible study. She wanted to be stamped a *Proven Woman!* That was the restart of the relationship they never had, but always wanted! This is the story of a man who once thought the best option was suicide!

Tim was finally finished running from reality. He was done pretending all was well. He trusted that he didn't need to escape into fantasy. He believed that the life God had for him would be sufficient. He trusted that he could be vulnerable and open with his wife, despite the pain that goes along with real relationships.

A New Worldview

Tim no longer believes the lies that he doesn't measure up or is no good. He is so overwhelmed by the love of the Lord that he cannot help but cry during prayer or worship times. Tim gave up self-medication of porn, alcohol and masturbating 10 times a day, to spending time meeting with the Lord.

Although it took Tim three times through the *Proven Men Study,* once it took hold, Tim never turned back. Sure, there were the occasional times when the old voice was telling him that he didn't deserve love that led to Tim retreating into masturbation, but Tim quickly ran back to the Lord.

Today, Tim has been leading support groups for more than five years. He is still quick to search out and find men who have low self-esteem so he can put his arms around them and share his story and his life.

If Tim can do it, so can you! Be on Guard. Live a Proven life.

STAN
Single and Sliding Down a Slippery Slope

Stan grew up in the church where his dad was the pastor. He attended a Christian college with the dream of making it in the music industry. He was well acquainted with Scriptures. College life was fun and he had lots of friends. Stan had time to play sports and attend parties. That's where he met Missy. Stan was nuts about her. Missy was so awesome and passionate for the Lord. She was definitely the one he planned to marry. In fact, he couldn't keep his hands off her. Their dates always turn steamy.

That's when Stan's two worlds began to collide and he knew he needed sexual integrity. His habit of masturbating to Internet porn suddenly caught up with him. All he can think about is making love with Missy. Will he be able to turn his thoughts away from sex to keep the girl of his dreams?

Clean Outside of the Cup

Stan had never really considered the possibility of living a Proven life. Growing up, Stan had had to memorize Scripture better than others, behave better than others, and sacrifice better than others. As a "PK" (pastor's kid), Stan lived in a glass house. But it wasn't all that bad. His parents remained married and loved him. Stan learned early that he received the most praise when he followed the rules or set an example. He excelled at putting on a good face. Stan was pleased to sing songs at church because everyone clapped and the older ladies would always give him praises. Everyone told his parents what a treasure they had in Stan.

Life was simple. It had one rule: Stay out of trouble. As long as no one complained to his dad, everything was good at home. Of course, Stan's dad was busy meeting everyone else's needs, which left little time for Stan. Therefore, Stan grew to entertain himself. Knowing that it's best not to let others see his inside, it didn't take too long for Stan to figure out the allure of Internet pornography and a fantasy life.

Every naked or scantily dressed woman in the pictures was wearing the same smile. You know the one—the ministry smile: "No matter what you feel inside, always smile and say everything is great." As Stan stared at the computer images of women smiling at him, Stan felt good. They made no demands of him. They were there to fulfill his every need and meet all of his desires. They never judged him nor demanded anything. It was perfect. Adding masturbation to the mix, he was hooked. Nothing felt so good. It made up for all the things he had to do to please everyone else. Even when doing the jobs at church his dad made him do because no one else would do them, Stan knew his private reward was waiting for him.

Marry Missy or Miss Out?

During college, when Stan began dating Missy, a new world opened to him. He was infatuated with her and she with him. They couldn't stand to be apart. Everything about her was fresh and exciting. Her touch was electric. Each stare increased his hormone level, so that when he was with Missy, all he could think about was unbuttoning her blouse. Deep down, Stan wanted purity, but the tug of the ecstasy of the moment was so hard to give up. Then one day he crossed the line. After that, neither he nor Missy could claim to be virgins even under the most liberal definition. It didn't take too long before Missy was feeling guilty. She was certain she would be a virgin when she married. Now that was lost—lost at the hands of Stan. Their relationship was crumbling. Stan feared she might break up with him.

Where could Stan turn? He couldn't tell his father that he is addicted to pornography or that he is having sex before marriage. His dad might call him before the elders for the laying on of hands. He was sure he would be judged by them if the sin didn't just go away once they prayed for him. In addition, there was never any sermon about sex or any other evidence that his dad or the church would realize that it takes time to change and heal. Stan had to figure out a solution himself. Fortunately, his skill with the computer landed him at the Proven Men website. All he had to do was join, but that would mean admitting his practices. It was a hard decision to make.

Lack of Intimacy with God

It took Stan a long time to see the love his Heavenly Father wanted to give him. Stan was filled with head knowledge, but never truly knew the power of the Scriptures or the meaning of a deep intimate relationship with God. Despite his upbringing in the church, he needed a spiritual heart transplant. Stan needed to actually trust in God and surrender his will for his future to the Lord. Being unable to stop having sexual contact with his beloved girlfriend was what it took for Stan to understand that God couldn't be bargained with and that true Christianity required total surrender.

Stan began reading testimonies and stories on the website of Proven Men about men—men just like himself. Contacting them seemed like a risk he could afford. After all, this way his dad and no one from church would even know about it—about his secrets. But it wasn't that easy. Stan still had to battle his pride. At first, Stan wondered why he should attend a dozen group meetings. He was not thrilled about adding yet another Bible study to his menu.

Stan certainly knew more about the Bible than the man leading. Ultimately, Stan decided to sign up because he knew he needed to do something, anything. After all, he wanted to keep Missy.

New Relationships with God

Stan figured that a confidential small group of men was a risk he could afford. Stan committed that he would work through the *Study*, and weekly join in accountability with others sharing the same struggle. After all, it was only for 12 weeks. He reminded himself that he could bail if it was too boring.

Something remarkable began to happen. Stan was able to share anything in that small group without a single person judging him. He didn't have to pretend to be perfect. This was new territory for Stan, so he stuck around.

After several weeks of going through the *Study*, Stan's heart began to melt. Tears even came to his eyes. He couldn't believe it. Stan had memorized Scripture for years, but had never known its true power or the real meaning of an intimate relationship with God. But now Stan was experiencing a new relationship with God.

One night at group he shook his head and told the leader, "I cannot believe it. The message of the Gospel is so simple. I finally get it." Stan was stunned at the simplicity of the Proven Path, how it really did capture the Christian walk. He had thought that his years of study would bring him closer to God, but only now was Stan yielding his life and beginning to live out the simple Gospel.

Stan wanted to be stamped PROVEN—not to earn a reward, but to know the Lord intimately. He now wanted to obey instead of play religion. Stan was committed to being open and honest, instead of posing. He wanted real relationships. He wanted to know God as a real person. Stan also began to recognize that sexual integrity was worth the price, that being faithful to the Lord was worth more than anything else. He was also beginning to understand that premarital sex hindered and damaged relationships, even after marriage. He wanted to know—truly know—Missy. And once he could accept that God was not holding out on him, it fortified him to wait for sex until he was married. He started to see that true intimacy must come first.

Time to Make a Choice

Stan began to love going to the Proven Men small groups each week. He was no longer in the glass house. It was safe to admit he was not perfect. At first, however, Stan was skeptical of the path. He already knew the Bible. In fact, he had gotten As in his college seminary courses. But he was starting to see how he had been like the Pharisees who knew the Bible without knowing the Lord. The simplicity of the Gospel was breaking his proud heart.

Yet, it wasn't all a bed of roses. Stan had formed a habit of turning to porn as his little treat for being so good. And then there was Missy. Every time he was with her, he burned with passion. It wasn't easy going backward in the physical part of their relationship. Having tasted the sweet water, it was hard not to return for it again. But he wanted to honor Missy. He wanted to start over, to have a second virginity. Equally important, he wanted to be a leader spiritually. Missy's consent to premarital sex didn't make it right. He wanted to be the knight, protecting the fair maiden.

It was good for Stan to listen to the stories of others in the group. The married men spoke of the damage pornography and even premarital sex had done to their marriages, many of which were just hanging on by a thread. It was also good to hear the same struggles among the single men. It was time for Stan to make a choice.

A Game Plan for Triggers

Stan used to love going to the gym. It was included in the price of college tuition. It wasn't clear whether it was a runner's high or sexual fantasy that made the treadmill so enjoyable. He always found a spot near the young ladies and allowed his eyes to enjoy the view of their firm bodies. He also was on the Internet daily, frequently to sites where seductively dressed women were featured, whether it was sporting news or the latest video on Youtube®.

If he made a list of places that fueled fantasy, Stan would add magazine racks, coffee houses, everywhere on college campus, and even church. His list of triggers included being bored and also the stress from juggling his classes, sports and even kissing Missy. The more he thought about it, the more he discovered that he was a budding sex addict.

Stan was not pleased to know how much of a foothold he gave to Satan when it came to fixating on sex in his daily life. He began making a game plan for each of the different places or triggers that enticed him. He knew he needed to do business with each one separately as they each had different attractions and different solutions. For instance, Stan decided not to go to the gym for a season because he couldn't keep his eyes from wandering. That place was just too great a temptation. He also put filters on his computer and never used the computer when he was alone. He would go to the school library to use it. While in the library, he also chose a desk that faced the wall, instead of ones where the ladies walked past.

The final frontier was what to do about Missy. This would prove to be his biggest challenge. His leader suggested that he make the hard choice of never being alone with Missy in his apartment or other places where they used to make out. Was that too radical? Was it truly necessary?

Sacred Sacrifice

Stan had known sacrifice. He had watched his pastor dad work 70 hours a week, sacrificing everything and receiving little in return. Stan was committed not to making the same mistake. Therefore, Stan was always on guard. He doubted everyone's motive. They only wanted something. At most, Stan was willing to risk his time, but not his heart in helping others.

Then along came Missy. He wanted her in his life. His goal was to marry her. He would win her on his own. Things had been great, until she started backing away due to her guilt over premarital sex. First, Stan tried to convince her it was okay, but that didn't work. Next, he relied upon his strength to fight temptation on their dates. It was a battle he couldn't win.

Although Stan couldn't see it at the time, losing the battle for purity was what it took to realize that he was a control freak. It was that need for control that kept God at a distance. Without enlisting God, Stan would not be pure. But God would not act as a vending machine. He didn't answer the purported prayers of Stan asking God to take away the temptations. The Lord was not interested in Stan just refraining from premarital sex, but wanted a real relationship with him. The good news is that Stan started seeing this himself. He was finally willing to open up to the Lord. He was willing to put down the shovel of self-effort.

Swinging the Sword for Absolute Purity

As you might expect from a young man in love, about the only thing on Stan's mind was marrying Missy. Of course, he had wanted some of those benefits now. Fortunately, Stan now realized that building a strong marriage begins while dating. He needed to protect Missy and protect his own sexual integrity.

As hard as it was for Stan to understand, he listened as married men in the group told him that their wives regretted premarital sex after they got married. They carried guilt forward into marriage and it often affected their sexual relations in marriage. Stan also listened as they shared that they too were not immune to the effects of pornography and fantasy. They warned Stan that he was training himself to compare Missy to all the fantasies he allowed in his mind. Each of them was competing against Missy. Stan didn't want to subconsciously compare them to her. Stan didn't want to usher into his marriage the typical male view that sexual relations with a spouse is just "sex," knowing that Missy would be longing for intimacy. In short, Stan knew he needed to swing the sword of the Spirit to fight for purity or he would put his future marriage at risk.

Ruining and Replacing

At every corner on campus, there was a pretty woman. Stan needed to take captive every thought and conform it to Christ. The three Rs were helpful to Stan. At first, it was amazing to realize just how much he was looking with lust at women. Dozens of times a day he caught himself daydreaming about sex or taking second looks. Stan was doing more than just looking—he was memorizing women's bodies, comparing or rating them in his mind. Sometimes his friends would even joke about what score to give a girl that walked by or would nudge him to take notice of someone.

Stan made a decision to stop allowing these thoughts to fill his mind. He began to practice "ruining and replacing." Each time he began thinking sexual thoughts about a woman, he would confess it as sin. During battles, he would constantly say to himself, "ruin and replace." Even as the thought tried to creep back in, Stan would not take any pleasure from it. Stan also began taking the Proven

Men weekly memory verses with him to aid him in the battle and to replace the daydreaming.

Stan also told his friends that he didn't want to listen to sexual jokes or play the rating game anymore. He was even brave enough to tell them that he was interested in purity and mentioned that he was attending a sexual integrity group. He told them he had given up pornography and was attending Proven Men meetings. He suggested that they check out the Proven Men website.

Building God into His Life

There were times in Stan's life where he used to suffer such a caustic reaction in his body when tempted to seek out Internet pornography that his stomach hurt. In those instances of intense attack, he eventually and always gave in. Although there was definitely spiritual warfare going on, the root issue was that pornography remained an option for him. Freedom from pornography arrived only when he made an irrevocable commitment that it's no longer an option. He finally realized that because pornography was an option, the intense desire raged on. It was only when his mind and body began accepting that never again would pornography be allowed, that they stopped begging for it. Of course, it was hard. He still had some stomach pain at first, but Stan would put his game plan in place, such as go jogging and flee the temptation. Stan also gave up Internet access on his cell telephone.

What about Missy? At first, Stan didn't want to make a commitment that heavy petting with his girlfriend was not an option. He justified it in many ways, such as they were going to get married anyway, and that what they were doing was not really pre-marital sex and that no one was getting hurt. But it was affecting their relationship. They both felt the weight of guilt. Finally, Stan took a stand for sexual integrity in this area. Premarital sex would not remain an option.

The evidence that Stan truly made this commitment was evident by what he did. He set limits on their dates, including never being alone with Missy. That's right, never alone with his fiancée! This was one of the hardest battles of his life. It was even harder for Stan than giving up pornography.

Stan wanted to be with Missy all the time, but the "never alone" rule was constricting. It was hard to always be in a group or in a public place. Yet Stan embraced that it was not about following a man-made rule, but that the Lord truly had something better for them. What they did prior to marriage did matter and affect their future marriage.

Stan also began deepening his reliance on and relationship with the Lord. In addition to his own "quiet time" with the Lord, on every date they would read the Bible together. He was actually building God into his life and future marriage, not just doing what Christians think they are supposed to do.

Married and Madly in Love

Stan has done the unthinkable. He went against the tidal wave of the world and stopped having premarital sex even though he was engaged to be married. It was hard, but it was no longer an option. Only when he was willing to stop being alone with Missy did he begin to win the battles. He also gave up pornography for good.

Stan is glad he suffered through it because he is now married and still madly in love with Missy. By jointly agreeing to put Christ first while dating, the transition to putting Him first while married was much easier. There are so many more battles in marriage that need this type of commitment, that they were glad for the early training.

With a child on the way, Stan is also grateful that he won't be passing down to his children a selfish lifestyle or sexual sins. He trusts God at his word that even though the sins of a selfish man are passed to the third and fourth generation, this cycle can be broken by turning to the Lord and receiving God's mercy and promise of showing love to a thousand generations of those who love and keep God's commandments.

Single men take heart and courage. Be on Guard. Live a Proven life.

Endnotes

[1] http://www.ncfpc.org/stories/080813s1.html (Prime-Time TV Glorifies Non-Marital Sex).

[2] id.

[3] Results of *MSNBC.com*, 2000 Online Cybersex Survey, printed by *Business Wire*, July 19, 2001.

[4] MSNBC/Stanford/Duquesne Study, printed by *The Washington Times* (1/26/2000).

[5] *Porn addiction is more than skin deep* by Editor: Kevin Axe, reprinted at http://www.faithlinks.org/viewarticle.asp?ID=550.

[6] *The Hart Report,* by Dr. Archibald D. Hart, printed in *The Sexual Man* by Dr. Archibald D. Hart, Word Publishing, 1994, page 119.

[7] id.

[8] id.

[9] *Men's Secret Wars*, by Pat Means, Revell, 1996, page 255.

[10] 2 Timothy 3:6.

[11] 1 Timothy 5:2.

[12] 2 Timothy 3:2–7.

[13] 1 Timothy 5:1–2.

[14] 2 Timothy 3:7.

[15] 1 Timothy 5:2.

[16] Ephesians 4:19–24, 5:3; Colossians 3:5–7; 1 Thessalonians 4:3–7.

[17] Matthew 5:28.

[18] 1 Samuel 16:7; Galatians 2:6.

[19] Matthew 6:24.

[20] The term "false intimacy" was presented in the book, *False Intimacy: Understanding the Struggle of Sexual Addiction*, by Dr. Harry Schaumburg (NavPress 1992).

[21] See Hebrews 13:4–5.

[22] Ephesians 4:19–24, 5:3–5.

[23] Romans 12:1–2.

[24] Colossians 2:20–23.

[25] Numbers 32:23.

[26] Proverbs 6:27.

[27] Luke 14:27.

[28] Luke 14:28–30.

[29] Luke 14:33.

[30] American Psychiatric Association (2000), *Diagnostic and statistical manual of mental disorders*, 4th Ed. It does, however, note that there exist sexual disorders, such as compulsive masturbation or compulsive sex in a relationship. See Irons, R.,& Schneider, J. P. (1996). Differential diagnosis of addictive sexual disorders using the DSM-IV. *Sexual Addiction & Compulsivity, 3*, 7–21.

[31] Carnes, P., & Adams, K. M. (2002). *Clinical management of sex addiction*. Psychology Press.

[32] *False Intimacy*, by Dr. Harry Schaumburg (NavPress 1992) (pages 22, 31, 38, 72, 80).

[33] Colossians 3:5: "Put to death, therefore, whatever belongs to your earthly nature: sexual immorality, impurity, lust, evil desires and greed, which is idolatry."

[34] Ephesians 2:3; 1 John 2:16.

[35] Ephesians 4:19.

[36] James 4:3.

[37] Most of the time, your anger is not righteous, and it leads to sin and harm. In short, the ground you plow is so hardened by anger that the land cannot yield the fruit of peace, joy, love, or forgiveness (compare Galatians 5:19–21 with Galatians 5:22–24).

[38] Romans 2:8–9.

[39] See 2 Corinthians 10:5 ("We demolish arguments and every pretension that sets itself up against the knowledge of God, and we take captive every thought to make it obedient to Christ.").

[40] Dear friend, repent because God warns that it is better for a huge rock to be tied around your neck and thrown into the sea than for you to participate in another person's fall (Luke 17:1–2).

[41] These all are the fruit of living according to the sinful nature. (See Galatians 5:19–21: "The acts of the sinful nature are obvious: sexual immorality, impurity and debauchery; idolatry and witchcraft; hatred, discord, jealousy, fits of rage, selfish ambition, dissensions, factions and envy; drunkenness, orgies, and the like.")

[42] Romans 12:1–2.

[43] Galatians 5:16.

[44] Colossians 3:6–6.

[45] http://www.parentstv.org/PTC/facts/mediafacts.asp.

[46] Ephesians 5:31.

[47] Over 40 percent of couples that live together do not end up getting married. "Co-habitating couples not likely to marry"; Sharon Sassler, http://researchnews.osu.edu/archive/cohabit.htm.

[48] Those that live together before marriage have a higher risk, between 40% to 85%, of divorce than those that do not. (Bumpass & Sweet 1995; Hall & Zhao 1995; Bracher, Stantow, Morgan & Russell 1993; DeMaris & Rao 1992 and Glen 1990).

[49] Journal of Psychology and Christianity.

[50] 2 Peter 2:14 (New Living Translation ©2007).

51 Titus 2:12.

52 Galatians 5:16.

53 This term was coined in the excellent book *Sexual Healing: God's Plan for the Sanctification of Broken Lives,* by Dr. David Kyle Foster (Mastering Life Ministries), p. 268.

54 Proverbs 27:17.

55 Colossians 2:20–23.

56 Psalms 127:1.

57 Matthew 4:10; see also Nehemiah 9:6; Psalms 99:5; John 4:23–24; Hebrews 12:28–29.

58 John 1:12; 1 John 3:1.

59 Ephesians 1:5.

60 James 2:23; John 15:15.

61 Webster's New World Dictionary, Third College Edition 1988.

62 Matthew 22:36.

63 Luke 18:9–14.

64 Matthew 22:36–40.

65 1 John 4:20.

66 1 Peter 1:16.

67 Pure Life Ministries (www.Purelifeministries.org) considers pride and selfishness to be root issues of sexual sin and likely used a similar hand analogy prior to use by Prove Men Ministries. Pure Life Ministries has been helping men break free from sexual sin for 25 years. The author went through its at-home program a decade ago, and that ministry had a great impact in his life at that time.

68 2 Timothy 4:3.

69 James 4:4–6.

70 1 Peter 5:5.

71 John 20:24–28.

72 Philippians 1:14–19; James 1:2–4.

[73]   Luke 9:23.

[74]   John 5:2–9.

[75]   Galatians 6:4.

[76]   Matthew 22:36–39.

[77]   Proverbs 6:27–28.

[78]   Colossians 2:20–23.

[79]   Matthew 12:43–45.

[80]   id.

[81]   Revelation 21:5.

[82]   Titus 2:13–15.

[83]   Matthew 14:28.

[84]   Matthew 16:22.

[85]   Matthew 16:24.

[86]   Matthew 26:69–75.

[87]   Matthew 26:13–15.

[88]   Matthew 27:3–5.

[89]   Ephesians 2:8–9.

[90]   Romans 8:35.

[91]   Revelation 21:5.

[92]   Titus 2:13–15.

[93]   This bicycle riding analogy is adapted from one used in *Sexual Healing*, p. 289.

[94]   2 Peter 1:5–10.

[95]   Colossians 2:20–23.

[96]   John 15:5.

[97]   Galatians 5:16.

[98]   Matthew 11:30.

[99]   2 Peter 1:3–4.

[100]   Proverb 26:11.

[101] Galatians 2:20.

[102] 1 John 5:3–4.

[103] Philippians 4:13; 2 Thessalonians 3:3; James 4:10.

[104] James 1:13–15.

[105] 1 John 3:16.

[106] See Galatians 5:16.

[107] 1 Thessalonians 5:16–18.

[108] Galatians 5:22–23.

[109] Ephesians 6:10–18.

[110] Ephesians 6:10–20.

[111] Hebrews 4:12.

[112] Galatians 5:16.

[113] Proverbs 9:14–18.

[114] Proverbs 6:27.

[115] James 4:4.

[116] 1 Corinthians 6:18.

[117] 1 Corinthians 6:19–20.

[118] 1 Corinthians 10:13.

[119] *Every Man's Battle: Winning the War on Sexual Temptation One Victory at a Time,* by Stephen Arterburn and Fred Stoeker (WaterBrook Press 2000), p. 125.

[120] 2 Corinthians 10:5.

[121] Matthew 12:43–45.

[122] 1 John 1:9 (emphasis added).

[123] Colossians 3:2–3.

[124] Philippians 4:8.

[125] Isaiah 50:10–11.

[126] Matthew 6:24.

[127] Joshua 5:1.

[128] Exodus 13:17–14:31.

129 Joshua 3:14–4:18.

130 Numbers 22.

131 Numbers 22–24.

132 Numbers 31:16.

133 Numbers 25:1–3.

134 Numbers 25:6.

135 Numbers 31.

136 Job 31:1.

137 James 1:22.

138 Deuteronomy 7:2.

139 Deuteronomy 20:16–18.

140 Judges 1:28.

141 Judges 2:1–3.

142 2 Corinthians 10:5.

143 2 Corinthians 11:23–27.

144 2 Corinthians 12:7–10.

145 Matthew 6:34.

146 Luke 9:23.

147 Matthew 11:29.

148 Matthew 11:29–30.

149 2 Corinthians 1:3–5.

150 id.

151 1 Corinthians 6:9–11.

152 Exodus 20:5–6.

153 2 Peter 3:17–18.

154 Revelation 21:27.

155 Romans 6:23.

156 1 Peter 2:22; Hebrews 4:15; 2 Corinthians 5:21.

157 1 John 1:9.

[158] John 1:12.

[159] Ephesians 6:12.

[160] Matthew 5:28.

[161] "Lust is antithetical to true love: it dehumanizes another person into an object of passion, leading us to act as if the other were a visual or emotional prostitute for our use." http://www.biblegateway.com/resources/commentaries/IVP-NT/Matt/Do-Not-Covet-Others-Sexually (The IVP New Testament Commentary Series).

[162] id.

[163] Matthew 6:22–23.

[164] Exodus 20:17.

[165] Philippians 4:19.

[166] 1 Corinthians 10:13.

[167] Galatians 5:16; 2 Peter 1:3–10; Jude 24.

[168] Romans 14:23.

[169] 2 Timothy 4:3.

[170] God draws near those who draw near to Him (James 4:8) and He gives grace to the humble (James 4:6)—those who acknowledge that He is God and that He is good.

[171] See 1 Timothy 4:2.

[172] Genesis 2:24; Ephesians 5:31.

[173] Titus 2:11–12.

[174] Hebrews 12:4.

[175] James 1:2–4.

[176] 1 Timothy 4:7.

[177] 1 Thesolonians 4:3–5.

[178] Titus 2:6.

[179] 2 Timothy 2:22; 1 Corinthians 6:18–20.

[180] Romans 13:14.

181   1 Peter 2:11; 1 Thesolonians 4:3–5.

182   Romans 12:1–2.

183   James 1:22.

CPSIA information can be obtained
at www.ICGtesting.com
Printed in the USA
FFOW05n0025060214